# HOW CAN I BE SURE I'M A CHRISTIAN?

## What the Bible Says About Assurance of Salvation

DONALD S. WHITNEY

NAVPRESS®

## OUR GUARANTEE TO YOU

We believe so strongly in the message of our books that we are making this quality guarantee to you. If for any reason you are disappointed with the content of this book, return the title page to us with your name and address and we will refund to you the list price of the book. To help us serve you better, please briefly describe why you were disappointed. Mail your refund request to: NavPress, P.O. Box 35002, Colorado Springs, CO 80935.

**For a free catalog**
of NavPress books & Bible studies call
1-800-366-7788 (USA) or 1-800-839-4769 (Canada).

**www.navpress.com**

The Navigators is an international Christian organization. Our mission is to advance the gospel of Jesus and His kingdom into the nations through spiritual generations of laborers living and discipling among the lost. We see a vital movement of the gospel, fueled by prevailing prayer, flowing freely through relational networks and out into the nations where workers for the kingdom are next door to everywhere.

NavPress is the publishing ministry of The Navigators. The mission of NavPress is to reach, disciple, and equip people to know Christ and make Him known by publishing life-related materials that are biblically rooted and culturally relevant. Our vision is to stimulate spiritual transformation through every product we publish.

NavPress is the publishing ministry of The Navigators. NavPress publications help believers learn biblical truth and apply what they learn to their lives and ministries. Our mission is to stimulate spiritual formation among our readers.

Library of Congress Catalog Card Number:
93-48664

ISBN-13: 978-0-89109-772-3
ISBN-10: 0-89109-772-4

Unless otherwise identified, all Scripture quotations in this publication are taken from the HOLY BIBLE: NEW INTERNATIONAL VERSION® (NIV®). Copyright ©1973, 1978, 1984 by International Bible Society. Used by permission of Zondervan Publishing House. All rights reserved. Other versions used include: the New American Standard Bible (NASB), © The Lockman Foundation 1960, 1962, 1963, 1968, 1971, 1972, 1973, 1975, 1977; The New Testament in Modern English (PH), J. B. Phillips Translator, © J. B. Phillips 1958, 1960, 1972, used by permission of Macmillan Publishing Company; and the King James Version (KJV).

Whitney, Donald S.
    How can I be sure I'm a Christian? : what the Bible says about assurance of salvation / Donald S. Whitney.
        p.    cm.
    Includes bibliographical references.
    ISBN 0-89109-772-4
    1. Assurance (Theology)—Biblical teaching.    2.-Salvation—Biblical teaching.    I. Title.
BS680.A86W45    1994
    234—dc20                                                                                        93-48664
                                                                                                            CIP

Printed in the United States of America

9 10 11 12 13 14 / 11 10 09 08 07

# CONTENTS

✝

*To him who is able to keep you from falling*
*and to present you before his glorious presence*
*without fault and with great joy—*
*to the only God our Savior*
*be glory, majesty, power and authority,*
*through Jesus Christ our Lord,*
*before all ages, now and forevermore! Amen.*
JUDE 24-25

*And to Laurelen Christiana Whitney,*
*for whom we waited so long.*
*May the Lord draw you to Himself someday*
*and give you assurance of salvation in Christ.*

# FOREWORD

Contemporary Christianity often makes a false dichotomy between *doctrinal* and *practical* truth—as if the word *doctrine* meant truth that is inherently academic, ineffectual, useless in real life. Such thinking is faulty, of course. All "practical" truth—if it is really truth at all—must be grounded in sound doctrine. And all doctrine—true or false—has inevitable practical consequences.

No doctrine is more immediately practical than the doctrine of assurance. In fact, questions about assurance are often what prompt new Christians to begin their study of Bible doctrine. Perhaps you have picked up this very book because you hope to find answers to your own doubts or confusion. If so, you have chosen a solid, biblical, readable, and altogether helpful resource for your study.

There are two extremes to be avoided in the matter of assurance. One is the error of settling for an assurance that comes too easily. This can lead to a shallow, false assurance and a fatal spiritual apathy. This false assurance is the bane of our age. At the other extreme is a chronic uncertainty that leads to a preoccupation with oneself, one's fears, and one's failings. It results in a vacillating, feeble faith. That tendency plagued the church in earlier ages, and sadly there are still whole denominations today where true, settled assurance is almost unheard of.

That God wants every believer to enjoy full assurance is clear in Scripture. The Apostle John wrote an entire epistle for this very purpose: "In order that you may know that you have eternal live" (1 John 5:13). The author of Hebrews wrote, "We desire that each one of you show the same diligence so as to realize the full assurance of hope until the end" (6:11), and "Let us draw near with a sincere heart in full assurance of faith" (10:22).

Assurance is therefore the birthright and privilege of every true believer in Christ. Yet virtually all Christians will testify that doubts assail our assurance from time to time. Knowing how to handle such doubts, understanding the self-examination that is required (2 Corinthians 13:5), discerning the evidences of Christ in us, and above all focusing our faith on the promises of Scripture and the character of God—those are the keys to maintaining true assurance.

Too many contemporary books on assurance treat the subject in an entirely superficial fashion. So eager are they to assure *everyone*, that they ignore the biblical warnings against false assurance. In contrast, some older books make assurance dependent on such high standards of personal holiness that they render real certainty virtually unattainable.

In *How Can I Be Sure I'm a Christian?* Don Whitney manages to steer a clear and steady course between the Scylla of smug false assurance and the Charybdis of brooding fixation on doubt. He shows a thorough familiarity with the complex doctrinal issues involved, yet he explains them simply and intelligibly in a way that makes these truths instantly accessible to all Christians. Best of all, he is thoroughly biblical throughout.

This is a rich and important work, which I am certain will be used greatly by God to help settle the assurance question for many who read it. Whether you are a new Christian seeking personal assurance at the outset of your walk with Christ or a seasoned Bible student hoping to deepen your understanding of a complex doctrine, I know you will find much here that will build you up, strengthen your faith, and enrich your spiritual understanding.

—JOHN MACARTHUR

# ACKNOWLEDGMENTS

The wisdom of Proverbs 11:14 teaches that "many advisers make victory sure." I want to acknowledge and thank (in alphabetical order) the "many advisers" provided by the Lord for this book. Most of these read all or part of the manuscript; all offered direction, suggestions, or encouragement: John Armstrong, Tom Ascol, Joel Beeke, Tim Beougher, John Blanchard, Jim Boice, D. A. Carson, Jim Elliff, Roger and Jean Fleming, R. F. Gates, Alan Griswood, Kent Hughes, T. W. Hunt, Phil Johnson, John MacArthur, Debbie Martens, Tom Nettles, Tom Phillips, Lance Quinn, Jim Sibley, Pat Stewart, and Ward Walker.

Thanks to Kate Sunday for the practical help on so many details.

Thanks to Jim Rahtjen for his willing spirit and for all the positive feedback.

Thanks to the people of NavPress for their thoroughness and author support.

Thanks to Jon Stine for being an editor who cares.

Thanks to the members of Glenfield Baptist Church for the love and prayer I needed during this project.

Special thanks to Caffy for believing in me.

Thank you all! And may God bless you for your role in the development of this book.

ONE

# ASSURANCE OF SALVATION— IS IT POSSIBLE?

———————— ✝ ————————

*Assurance is a precious gift, which many
that live in these days do undervalue, and tread under foot.*
ANDREW GRAY
*The Works of Andrew Gray*

In 1858, the steamship *Austria* caught fire and sank in the Atlantic, killing 400 people. One survivor told how he and five Christian friends stood between the fire behind them and the water before them. They agreed that at the end they would leap from the sinking ship together. When the time arrived, they joined hands, looked at each other, and just before jumping into the cold waters of the Atlantic, expressed their confidence that in just a few moments they would all meet in Heaven.[1]

The story greatly affected those in the prayer meeting where it was first told, and it had a powerful effect on me when I read it. What a beautiful way to meet death. What a joyful thought to imagine entering Heaven in a matter of minutes with an entire group of friends or loved ones. But most of all, what a wonderful thing it is, at the very moment of death, to have such strong confidence that you are going to Heaven.

When you think about the reality that each of us is going to die, there isn't anything more important than knowing whether you are going to Heaven.

Most people think they are going to Heaven. Researcher George Barna, in his book *What Americans Believe*, says 99 percent of Americans believe they're Heavenbound. When read the statement "When you die, you will not go to Heaven," only one in a hundred agreed.[2]

But the Bible disagrees. Jesus used the words *many* and *few* in a way that indicates that most people will not go to Heaven. As Matthew 7:13-14 records, He said, "Enter through the narrow gate. For wide is the gate and broad is the road that leads to destruction, and many enter through it. But small is the gate and narrow the road that leads to life, and only a few find it."

Obviously, many who think they are going to Heaven are mistaken. How can we avoid being deceived? Is there any way we can know *now* where we stand? Is it possible for us to have assurance like the people on the *Austria* did?

## IT IS POSSIBLE, INDEED NORMAL, FOR THE CHRISTIAN TO EXPERIENCE ASSURANCE OF SALVATION

Assurance of salvation is a God-given awareness that He has accepted the death of Christ on your behalf and forgiven you of your sins. It involves confidence that God loves you, that He has chosen you, and that you will go to Heaven. Assurance includes a sense of freedom from the guilt of sin, relief from the fear of judgment, and joy in your relationship with God as your Father.

Unfortunately, many people don't believe assurance of salvation is possible in this world. (Some allow for the possibility if you are one of the extremely rare "saints" to whom God gives an unusual, extra-biblical revelation that you are saved.) They teach that, despite your earnest response to all you've been taught from Scripture, you must continue to live under the shadow of discovering at the Judgment that you are not saved. In the official teachings of at least one large group, curses are heaped upon those who say you may know in this life that you are right with God, your sins are forgiven, and you are going to Heaven.

But assurance of salvation is not only *possible*, it should be the *normal* experience for every Christian.

Romans 8:16 boldly declares, "The Spirit himself testifies with our spirit that we are God's children." That describes an ongoing, present-tense experience that is normative for the children of God. The assurance of salvation the Apostle Paul had should be the experience of every Christian: "I know whom I have believed, and am convinced that he is able to guard what I have entrusted to him for that day" (2 Timothy 1:12).

In 2 Peter 1:10 God actually *commands* us to pursue the assurance of our salvation: "Therefore, brethren, be all the more diligent to make certain about His calling and choosing you" (NASB). He would not command every Christian to make this pursuit of certainty unless He intended to give certainty.

Clearest of all is 1 John 5:13. There the Apostle John tells us that the very reason he wrote that letter was so that those who believe in Jesus Christ would *know* that they have eternal life: "I write these things to you who believe in the name of the Son of God so that you may know that you have eternal life."

Some teach that assurance is of the essence of faith, that is, a part of genuine faith. You haven't really come to believe in Christ, they contend, unless you are *sure* you are saved by Christ. They point to passages like Hebrews 11:1, which says, "Now faith is being sure of what we hope for and certain of what we do not see." Obviously, there must be at least some degree of certainty in the power and willingness of Christ to save you, or else you would not believe in Him to do so. But how much certainty is necessary? Some saved people will have strong assurance from the beginning, but not all do.

We must not say that firm, unshakable assurance is necessary for salvation to be real. You can be a true Christian without having a powerful sense of assurance. If that were not so, the Apostle John would not have said in 1 John 5:13 that he was writing to people he knew to be believers so that they would *know* that they had eternal life.

Even if we grant that some measure of assurance is intrinsic to faith, the Bible never emphasizes this when it tells us how to be saved. Instead it tells us (in Mark 1:15, for example) that we must repent and believe to become Christians. It does not say to repent, believe, *and* have assurance. So if there is a kind of assurance that is inherent to faith itself, it is different from what Hebrews 10:22 calls the "*full* assurance of faith" (emphasis added). Between these two points are *degrees* of assurance.

While the Bible does not require an unflinching, fully developed assurance of salvation for a person to be a Christian, it does tell us that it is possible—in fact, normal—for a Christian to enjoy a rich and satisfying assurance.

Think of it this way. If a governor pardons a death-row criminal, he will tell him. He will not force the condemned man to wait until his neck is in the noose to inform him he is pardoned. Likewise, when God pardons us and adopts us into His family, He does not want to hide our new status from us until the moment we stand quivering before Him, wondering if a trapdoor over hell is about to open beneath our feet. He wants us to know we're pardoned and to confidently "draw near . . . with a sincere heart in full assurance of faith" (Hebrews 10:22).

## IT IS POSSIBLE, INDEED NORMAL FOR A NONCHRISTIAN TO HAVE A FALSE ASSURANCE OF SALVATION

While many who doubt their salvation shouldn't, there are also many who *don't* doubt their salvation who *should.*

Speaking of the Day of Judgment, Jesus said, "Many will say to me on that day, 'Lord, Lord, did we not prophesy in your name, and in your name drive out demons and perform many miracles?' Then I will tell them plainly, 'I never knew you. Away from me, you evildoers!'" (Matthew 7:22-23). Many will be shocked when they aren't accepted. Until that moment they will be confident— they have assurance—but it's a false assurance.

Remember the Barna survey—99 percent believe they are going to Heaven.

There was a prominent religious group in Jesus' day who had a false assurance. They were called the Pharisees, a scrupulously religious sect of the Jews. They were invariably at odds with the teaching of Jesus, but they were quite sure they were right with God. They would brazenly pray, "God, I thank you that I am not like other men—robbers, evildoers, adulterers—or even like this tax collector. I fast twice a week and give a tenth of all I get" (Luke 18:11-12).

Their assurance, however, was not based upon truth. Despite their veneer of righteousness and obedience to God's commands, Jesus reserved His most withering words for them, such as "son of hell" and "How will you escape being condemned to hell?" (Matthew 23:15,33).

A "son of hell" can feel quite secure and assured that he is bound for Heaven, even up to the moment of condemnation. How can this be? We will pick this up later, but for now, let's briefly note a few contrasts between true Christians and falsely assured professing Christians. Christians are fearful of sinning away their assurance. Believers know, usually by experience as well as by doctrine, that sometimes assurance atrophies as the result of sin. They will prize assurance enough to protect it. Spuriously assured persons, however, are usually unconcerned about the potential loss of assurance. Casual and nonchalant would describe their attitude toward assurance. They simply take their assurance for granted.

Another difference is that people with pseudoassurance turn first to other things for assurance rather than to the Word of God. As in Matthew 7:22-23, those surprised by condemnation at the Judgment do not say something like, "Lord, You promised in Your Word that if we would repent and believe You would receive us." Instead, they will base their confidence upon their prophesyings, exorcisms, and miracles. If such people are reminded today that Scripture should be the primary source of assurance, they would quickly say, "Oh yes, yes, of course I agree." But face to face with Christ Himself, they prove what they rely on by turning to things other than the promises of Scripture for their assurance.

How many people today, if asked why they are sure of their salvation, would answer, "I was baptized," or "I was confirmed," or "I go to church," or "I walked forward at the end of a church service," or "I prayed a prayer with someone," or "I was raised in a Christian home," or "I raised my hand in response to a sermon," or "I take the Lord's Supper" or "I did so many good things to help people"? These are essentially identical to the answer Jesus said would be given by many at the Judgment. These people reflect an illusional assurance based upon something done by man rather than something said and done by God.

Similarly, others are wrongly assured that they are right with God because of what they have *not* done. Like the Pharisee mentioned in Luke 18:11-12, they are self-confident before God because they are "not like other men—robbers, evildoers, adulterers." Most people understand why a Hitler or a mass murderer shouldn't be in Heaven, but unless they are notoriously wicked (and virtually no one thinks he or she is), they can't imagine God closing the door of eternity in *their* face. So while some have sham assurance thinking they *are so good*, others feel spiritually smug thinking they *aren't so bad*.

As we will see later, assurance does involve examining ourselves for evidence of Christlike actions, but the first place a Christian should turn for assurance is the Bible. Our confidence is not in ourselves, but in God and His Word. The message of Christ and salvation is in the Scriptures; that should be our primary source of assurance that we know the Christ and have the salvation revealed in the Scriptures.

Jesus' encounters with those in His day who had false assurance show us that it also breeds pride. The Pharisees seethed with an arrogant presumption of righteousness. Their spiritual conceit came from a self-conceived belief that they had earned the favor of God. Our own day has seen manifestations of arrogance from people under the same delusion of wrongly based assurance. Cult leader David Koresh was so egotistical about his place in Heaven that he sometimes signed letters as "Yahweh Koresh," audaciously taking an Old Testament name of God as his own. Many who would strongly denounce both the Pharisees and Koresh, however, think in ways similarly presumptuous, because they believe they need no other spiritual direction beyond their own ideas. Some are so prideful about their spiritual condition that they refuse to recognize their own potential for unfounded assurance or self-deception.

If you have true assurance though, the result is different.

When your assurance is nurtured by the knowledge that your heart and life have been changed by *God*, and that Heaven is yours solely because of what *He* has done, you have an alternate attitude. You aren't as prideful as those whose assurance mistakenly lounges upon what *they* have or have not done.

The Bible urges us to make sure we know Christ and are right with God, but it also warns us not to have a false sense of security. So it is important not only to have assurance of salvation, but also to know *why* you have it.

## MORE APPLICATION

*Do you believe in the reality of assurance of salvation?* The first step in gaining assurance of salvation is to believe that it exists. You may be, or have been, part of a church tradition which denies that once you become a Christian you can be sure you are a child of God. The turning point in the entire matter for you may be right here. Read 1 John 5:13 again. It plainly says, "You may know that you have eternal life." Do you believe that?

Or you may need to believe in the reality of assurance on a more personal level. Will you believe, not just that God does save people and that He does give assurance to some, but that it is possible for *you* to have assurance of salvation? Even though you may not have it now, will you believe *it is possible* to have confidence that God has accepted you?

*Do you believe in the importance of assurance of salvation?* You may believe in the reality of assurance, but does the concept compel you? Do you believe it is a critical matter? Do you say to yourself, "I *must* be sure of my salvation," or can you be content without strong assurance? Unlike the unbeliever, the person who knows Christ will realize that possessing the assurance of knowing Christ is not an incidental issue.

*Do you believe in the pursuit of assurance of salvation?* If you do believe that assurance is possible and important, then pursue it! Suppose you were on the brink of bankruptcy when an attorney called and notified you that you might be the heir of an unexpected fortune. You would do whatever was necessary to discover your standing in the matter. With such potential offered to you, especially at that time, you would be a great fool not to probe the opportunity. In the same way, if you really understand the availability and value of assurance, you will pursue it.

A famous nineteenth-century British preacher, C. H. Spurgeon, stressed this in his sermon "Assurance Sought":

> I can understand a man doubting whether he is truly converted or not, but I cannot countenance his apathy in resting quiet till he has solved the riddle. . . . How can you give sleep to your eyelids till you have known it? Not know whether you are in Christ or not; perhaps unreconciled, perhaps condemned already; perhaps on the brink of hell, perhaps with nothing more to keep you out of [hell] than the breath that is in your nostrils, or the circulating drop of blood which any one of ten thousand haps or mishaps may stop, and then your career is closed—your life-story ended . . . I entreat thee, I beseech thee, shake off this sluggishness. Ask the Lord to say unto thy soul tonight, "I am thy salvation." He is able, and He is willing; . . . He will do it for you when you eagerly seek it from Him.[3]

One day you will stand on the edge of death, just as those six men on the *Austria* did. When your turn comes to jump into eternity, where will you land? Do you have the assurance that you will land in Heaven? God is willing for all of His children to have that assurance. Are you willing to pursue it?

---

NOTES

1. Samuel Prime, *The Power of Prayer* (1859; reprint, Edinburgh: The Banner of Truth Trust, 1992), page 160.
2. George Barna, *What Americans Believe* (Ventura, CA: Regal, 1991), pages 198-199.
3. C. H. Spurgeon, "Assurance Sought," *Metropolitan Tabernacle Pulpit*, vol. 63 (London: Passmore and Alabaster, 1917; reprint, Pasadena, TX: Pilgrim Publications, 1980), page 21.

TWO
# HAVING DOUBTS
# ABOUT YOUR SALVATION
———————— ✞ ————————

*Our knowledge of God, of Christ, of ourselves,*
*and of the blessed Scripture . . . is imperfect in this life.*
*And how then can our assurance be perfect?*
THOMAS BROOKS
*The Works of Thomas Brooks*

Charles Haddon Spurgeon was a British Baptist preacher who began his London ministry as a nineteen-year-old in 1854 and remained in the same pastorate until his death at age fifty-seven. He was a phenomenon. Long before the modern mega-church, 6,000 people crowded every service to listen to him preach. No building seemed large enough to hold the masses that wanted to hear him. When he was only twenty-seven he preached to 23,654 at the Crystal Palace—without amplification. Sometimes he had to ask the members of his church not to attend on the following Sunday so that newcomers might find a seat. Once in 1879, the entire congregation left so that newcomers waiting outside could enter, and still every seat was claimed.

Spurgeon's messages were printed in newspapers and individually, with sales of single copies running up to 25,000 per week. His collected sermons fill sixty-three thick volumes, the largest set of books by a single author in the history of Christianity. *Christian History* magazine asserts that "Spurgeon is history's most widely read preacher (apart from biblical ones). Today, there is available more material written by Spurgeon than by any other Christian author, living or dead."[1] If evangelical pastors were surveyed as to their choice for the greatest preacher since biblical times, Charles Spurgeon would almost certainly be selected.

## IT IS POSSIBLE, INDEED NORMAL, FOR CHRISTIANS TO HAVE OCCASIONAL DOUBTS ABOUT THEIR SALVATION

Surely a man of God with such a singular impact on millions for decades would never doubt that he was a Christian. But in his autobiography, Spurgeon wrote of just such a battle: "I felt at that time very weary, and very sad, and very heavy at heart; and I began to doubt in my own mind whether I really enjoyed the things which I preached to others." Despite his incredible influence, he wondered if he was an outsider to the Kingdom of God. "It seemed to be a dreadful thing for me to be only a waiter, and not a guest, at the gospel feast." [2]

If Spurgeon experienced occasional doubts about his salvation, then the less gifted should not consider themselves strange for struggling with doubts. I've had them. And I've met very, very few Christians—well-known or unknown—who claim they've never questioned the veracity of their faith. Spurgeon said, "I have known one or two saints of God who have rarely doubted their interest [in Christ] at all." [3] *You are not abnormal if you have occasional doubts about whether you are a Christian.*

As mentioned in the previous chapter, the stated purpose of the letter of 1 John is to give assurance (see 5:13). Since this epistle was written to people the Apostle John believed to be Christians, and written to assure *them* that they had eternal life, it is implied that it's possible to genuinely believe in Christ and not have assurance of salvation. Therefore, it is not impossible for a true Christian to have at least occasional doubts.

### Doubting Assurance Is Not Unbelief

Remember that doubt is not the same as unbelief. Imagine one of those seemingly rare Christians who says he has never had a single doubt about the reality and safety of his relationship with Christ. Now suppose some critic of Christianity confronts him with what he (mistakenly) thinks is a contradiction in the Bible and says, "If the Bible contradicts itself about this, how can you be sure it's true when it speaks of Heaven, eternal life, etc.?"

Our brother may be completely unprepared for this challenge. As he wonders what an informed response might be, he may even entertain for a moment the possibility that the critic is correct and consider the implications of such an outcome. His bit of *doubt* is qualitatively different from the critic's *unbelief.* (Note that even as he entertains this question, he may still have assurance that he believes biblically in Christ but not be perpetually free from every vestige of doubt.)

Unbelief is unambiguous in its denial of certain things and clear about where it stands. Doubt is by definition unsure of its position. But doubt may lean in one of two directions. It may be skeptical doubt leaning away from faith and toward unbelief, or doubt that is straining toward faith but lacking in something. Often what is lacking is a more thorough understanding of the truth. As pieces of the truth increasingly fall into place, they are wholeheartedly embraced.

I write this book with the assumption that many who read it are leaning toward the truth and want to believe. In fact, they are reading it precisely because they want assurance that they do believe. Many, I trust, will find in these pages a clearer understanding of the truth of salvation and assurance.

## The Causes of Doubt Are Many
Although it is normal for a real Christian to have occasional doubts about being a real Christian, not every believer doubts his or her salvation for the same reasons. Sometimes the doubt comes because of unrepentant sin. Sin grieves the Holy Spirit, and since He is the One who gives us the experience of assurance, when we grieve Him we may temporarily lose our assurance. Sometimes spiritual indolence is the cause. Sometimes Satan accuses us and plants doubts in our minds. Sometimes the pressure of trials or harsh circumstances drives us to doubt our relationship with the Lord. Sometimes we may doubt merely because of our physical or mental condition at the time. Sometimes God withdraws a conscious sense of His presence from us (and with it a sense of assurance), even though we may

not have caused it by sin, so that we might learn to walk by faith and not by feelings or sight.

## Spiritual Immaturity May Contribute to Doubts About Assurance

If my pastoral observations are correct, the more recently you have come to Christ, the more likely you are to have doubts about your salvation. That's because you have less knowledge of the Word and ways of God than the mature. As your grasp of Scripture strengthens, so will the strength of your assurance. As you understand more of what God did for you in Christ, you will understand more of your true position before God in Christ. Also, the more you see God do in and through you, the more confident you will become of His saving grace in you.

## Sensitivity to Sin May Cause Confusion About Assurance

New believers especially doubt their salvation because they misunderstand their new sensitivity to sin. They have been given new vision into both righteousness and sin. The Bible says that "the god of this age has blinded the minds of unbelievers" (2 Corinthians 4:4). Not only do new believers see the things of God as never before, but they see sin more clearly. Now they are starkly aware of previously unperceived sins. They would have admitted to seeing a few sins in their lives before salvation, but with their new eyes they seem to discover them everywhere.

If new Christians don't understand why this is happening, they may think they're not Christians at all. At first they felt clean, new, and forgiven, but now they feel sin-infested.

Do you feel this way? If so, don't panic. You should be encouraged to know that *this new sensitivity to sin is actually one of the best signs that you are a Christian*. It is extremely unlikely that you would have any such concern unless the Holy Spirit was working within you. Why weren't you so concerned about your sin *before* you wanted to repent and come to Christ? It's because you were without the One who makes you concerned about it (cf. 1 Corinthians 2:14). The *Holy* Spirit's presence in a person makes that person sensitive to what is *not holy* within him or her. Until He enters us, we are blind to all but our most obvious sins.

## Comparison with Other Christians May Cloud Assurance

New Christians also make themselves susceptible to doubts about their assurance when they compare themselves to more mature Christians. An apple tree in our backyard began to bear fruit during our first year in our present home. But it didn't bear nearly as much fruit as it has in succeeding years. New Christians should realize that just as a new tree isn't as fruitful as a more mature one, so too new Christians shouldn't expect to see as much visible evidence of the new life within them as they see in believers with longer and deeper roots.

When you grieve over what you have not yet become, it often helps to remember how far you *have* come. What were you like before you professed faith in Christ? If there is biblical evidence that since then Christ has changed your life, don't lose your assurance over the appearance of more or deeper changes in the lives of others.

## Childhood Conversion Affects the Assurance of Some

Besides new believers, there's one other category of Christians that seems particularly vulnerable to doubts. I have found that the younger in life a person was converted, the more likely he or she is later to doubt the veracity of that conversion.

We will discuss this pattern in more detail in a later chapter, but one reason for it is that people who have been Christians since childhood—as I have been—know little else but being a Christian. You may not have seen the dramatic changes that sometimes accompany the lives of adult converts. When your Christian experience is basically the only life you've ever known, sometimes you wonder if the *only* thing you have known is the *real* thing.

Again, occasional anxiety like this is normal. It is spiritually healthy to have such concerns, for it reveals a concern the unconverted do not have—an eagerness "to make your calling and election sure" (2 Peter 1:10). The hearts of the unconverted are calloused, not sensitive to these things. They usually have a false sense of security and see no need for looking so intently into the state of their soul, while the Christian may think, "Could I be self-deceived? Lord, please don't let it be so. If I've made a mistake somehow in thinking I'm saved, I want to know. If I've never repented and believed before, I want to know." Do these kinds of uncertainties and longings occasionally mingle in your heart? If so, you have reason to hope and to be encouraged.

## MORE APPLICATION

*Experiencing chronic doubts about salvation is unusual.* While it is normal for a true Christian to experience unsettling doubts about the validity of his or her salvation, it is *not* normal to have *chronic* doubts about salvation. Occasional doubts— even horrifying doubts—are one thing, but doubts that persist in the face of every biblical remedy demand careful attention.

No one can set a length of time or depth of feeling that defines or distinguishes such doubts. They defy quantification. But we can say that unrelenting doubt is not a normal part of biblical Christianity. One explanation for such pernicious doubts must be faced squarely: They may indicate there is no salvation, regardless of past profession or practice. That's why . . .

*Taking all doubts about salvation seriously is important.* Nothing is more serious than judgment and eternity, Heaven and hell. Nothing is more perilous than risking your readiness for them. Doubts about your salvation must be confronted.

Until you address your lack of assurance and its cause, you'll have little joy and probably a lot of spiritual misery. You'll be spiritually ineffective and a poor testimony to others of what Christ does when He saves someone. I want to encourage you in your doubts, but more than that I want to encourage you *out* of your doubts.

*Removing occasional doubts about salvation is possible.* Christians are not at the mercy of their doubts. Armed with the truth of God's Word and the power of God's Spirit, every Christian has weapons that "have divine power to demolish strongholds" of doubt (2 Corinthians 10:4).

These doubt-demolishing weapons at your disposal are the same ones Spurgeon found powerfully effective. During the low ebb of his assurance, he attended church in a town in the English countryside one Sunday. The man who conducted the service that day was not an experienced preacher, but an engineer. He read the Scriptures, prayed, and then preached. Instead of developing his own message, however, and unaware of the identity of the visitor, he preached one of Spurgeon's own sermons! Nevertheless, Spurgeon later wrote, "The tears flowed freely from my eyes; I was moved to the deepest emotion by every sentence of the sermon, and I felt all my difficulty removed, for the gospel, I saw, was very dear to me, and had a wonderful effect upon my own heart."

When Spurgeon introduced himself afterward, the embarrassed man confessed, "Why, it was one of your sermons that I preached this morning!"

"Yes," replied the great preacher, "I know it was; but that was the very message that I wanted to hear, because I then saw that I did enjoy the very Word I myself preached."[4] God fortifies and enriches our assurance with the same material out of which He built its foundation—His Word and His Spirit.

NOTES
1. "Did You Know?" *Christian History*, vol. 10, issue 29, no. 1 (1991), page 2.
2. C. H. Spurgeon, *Autobiography, Volume 2: The Full Harvest, 1860-1892*, comp. Susannah Spurgeon and Joseph Harrald, rev. ed., 2 vols. (Edinburgh: The Banner of Truth Trust, 1973), page 365.
3. C. H. Spurgeon, "I Know That My Redeemer Liveth," *Metropolitan Tabernacle Pulpit*, vol. 9 (London: Passmore and Alabaster, 1864; reprint, Pasadena, TX: Pilgrim Publications, 1970), page 212.
4. Spurgeon, *Autobiography*, page 366.

# THREE

# THE BASIS OF ASSURANCE
— ✝ —

*Those who have had the most abiding assurance of God's love,*
*are those who have been most in meditation*
*on the written assurances of that love.*
J. W. ALEXANDER
*Consolation*

Jim, a man in our church, was talking with his neighbor recently when their conversation turned to spiritual things. "When you die," Jim asked pointedly, "if God were to ask you why He should let you into Heaven, what would you say?"

The neighbor hesitated. Like almost all Americans, he considered himself a future citizen of Heaven. But it was obvious that up to that point he had thought of his entrance into eternity as somehow automatic and probably had never imagined a scenario like Jim described. Finally an answer stumbled out, beginning with the words "Because I. . . ." Without describing the details, I can tell you that his answer was unbiblical. It was the kind of reply that will draw a terrible, shocking response from God at the Judgment and haunt millions in eternity forever.

Nearly everyone's answer to this question begins with "Because I," followed by phrases like, "led a good life," "prayed to receive Christ," "attended church," "was baptized," "tried to keep the Ten Commandments," "lived by the Golden Rule," "had a spiritual experience," "helped others," etc.

How would *you* answer that classic question? Would your response begin with "Because I . . ."? If so, your assurance may be built on a foundation of sand. Regardless of how the sentence is finished, most answers beginning with "Because I . . ." are really the same answer. They all reflect confidence in the same flimsy foundation, a foundation that will crumble into hell on the Day we stand before God.

We must begin by looking for assurance in the right places.

Where do we find out about God and the things of God in the first place? How do we know what we know about Him, salvation, and eternal life? What tells us about Jesus Christ and His life, death, and resurrection? Where do we get information about Heaven and how to get there? We are told about these things in the *Bible*. Then where should we look for *assurance* regarding them? In God's Word, the Bible.

## THE ASSURANCE OF SALVATION RESTS PRIMARILY ON THE CHARACTER OF GOD, THE WORK OF JESUS CHRIST, AND THE TRUTH OF GOD'S PROMISES

Our confidence that we are going to Heaven shouldn't be based upon a hope that begins with "Because I . . ." but on one that begins with "Because *God*. . . ."

### Assurance of Salvation Rests on the Character of God

Believers in Christ can be assured of salvation because God is perfect and good.

The Apostle Paul expressed a steadfast assurance of his salvation in 2 Timothy 1:12. Notice where he placed his confidence: "I know whom I have believed, and am convinced that he is able to guard what I have entrusted to him for that day." He relied not on what he had done, but on *whom* he had believed. His assurance rested on the character of God; he was convinced that *God* was altogether good and able to preserve his salvation for the Day of Judgment.

God is perfect. He has perfect wrath toward the unrepentant, but He has perfect love for those who are willing to turn from their sins and come to Him. He is the perfect Judge, but He is also perfectly merciful. Will the Lord, who is *perfectly* merciful, reject anyone—including you—who seeks Him? How could He coldly ignore you and still be perfect? How could He turn you away when Jesus said, "Whoever comes to me I will never drive away" (John 6:37)? Since Jesus was merciful to all who came to Him and rejected no one who sincerely wanted Him, you can have assurance that His tenderly merciful Father has not rejected you if you've asked Him for His Spirit.

Incidentally, because of the infallible character of God, you can also be sure that your relationship with Him is not a temporary one. Paul made this point in Philippians 1:6—"He who began a good work in you will carry it on to completion until the day of Christ Jesus." In His perfect love and unchanging mercy, God will not receive you today and reject you tomorrow. He did not begin the "good work" of making you like Christ without the ability or willingness to "carry it on to completion." (For more on the perseverance of God in protecting and preserving His people in faith, see John 3:16, 5:24, 6:35-40, 10:27-30; Romans 8:29-30,35,38-39; 1 Corinthians 1:8-9; 1 Thessalonians 5:23-24; Hebrews 10:14; Jude 1,24.)

## Assurance of Salvation Rests on the Work of Jesus Christ

We can also be assured of our salvation because of what God has done in the work of Jesus Christ.

In His death Christ didn't just make salvation *possible* for us. He *actually saved* those who believe in Christ (Colossians 1:13-14). Assurance thrives when we recognize that God accomplished something on our behalf in the cross of Jesus Christ.

God did not rescue "the Son he loves" from the cross because, through Jesus' death, God was rescuing *us*. While God was bringing darkness over Jerusalem during the Crucifixion, He was bringing us into His Kingdom of Light. As Jesus bled, God was paying the price for our redemption from sin's guilt. With the death of Christ, "the forgiveness of [our] sins" became a fact to the Father. If you love "the Son he loves," assurance can be a settled matter for you because of what God perfected for your sake through the work of Christ.

Remember that God sent Christ (who willingly came) to the earth for a *purpose*. In oneness with the desires and design of the Father, Jesus descended from His throne in Heaven and entered a stable in Bethlehem. But He didn't just drop in for a royal visit, Jesus came on a mission: "He will save his people from their sins" (Matthew 1:21).

An important question for you now is, "Did Jesus accomplish His mission?" Read that question again. You can't say no without condemning to hell every person who's ever lived. If Jesus failed to "save his people from their sins," then there is no salvation. Do you realize, however, that if you say that Jesus only made salvation *possible*—rather than believing that Jesus actually saved His people from their sins—then that also means He did not fulfill the objective of His coming?

Paul proclaims in 1 Timothy 1:15 that "Christ Jesus came into the world to save sinners," and He did save them! Mission accomplished! Because He fully accomplished it, "there is now no condemnation for those who are in Christ Jesus" (Romans 8:1), and assurance is offered to all His people.

We begin experiencing the salvation Jesus accomplished when we believe that because of His death God forgives our sins and gives us eternal life. Such faith in Jesus Christ and His work involves believing with your head, your heart, and your life. No one can believe in the message about Christ unless he or she first hears it (Romans 10:14). So faith begins with hearing the Bible's message about the death and resurrection of Jesus for sinners and accepting that message as truthful. Thus, no one is a Christian who just "believes in God" and has had a meaningful "spiritual experience." People are saved by Christ only if they hear about and believe in *Christ*.

There are millions, however, who are not true Christians but accept all the biblical facts about Jesus Christ as truthful. Luke's words remind us that even demons publicly admitted to Jesus, "'You are the Son of God!' . . . because they knew he was the Christ" (Luke 4:41). I can acknowledge that George Washington was the first U.S. president and accept all the biographies about him as true, without placing faith in or relying upon the man.

There's more to faith in Christ than mental assent to the details of His life and miraculous power. In John 2:23-25 people accepted the facts about Jesus' power. They regarded all they had seen and heard about Him as true and from God. But Jesus knew what was in their hearts. He knew that their faith, which was commendable as far as it went, was not fully formed. So He did not "entrust himself to them." He did not become theirs as Savior.

Real faith in Christ includes believing with the *heart* as well as the head. To believe in Christ with the heart means trusting Him to save you from the guilt of your sin and to make you right with God. It means believing that you have no hope of being accepted by God on your own, but that God will receive you because of what Jesus has done on your behalf. Heart faith in Jesus Christ sincerely cries out to Him in prayer for salvation (Romans 10:13). The motive of your cry is not merely to obtain an insurance policy against hell, or to please someone else, or to strike a deal with God, but to find forgiveness and a relationship with Him.

We are saved by God's grace through faith in Christ alone (Ephesians 2:8-9), but not by a faith that is alone. "What good is it, my brothers," asked James, "if a man claims to have faith but has no deeds? Can such faith save him?" (James 2:14). Doing the will of the "Father who is in heaven," as Jesus referred to good deeds, is *not* needed for salvation, but it is needed *afterward* to *demonstrate* the *genuineness* of salvation. "Faith by itself," James explains, "if it is not accompanied by action, is dead" (2:17). In other words, even though a person thinks he believes in Christ, if he has no new attitude of obedience toward the will of Christ and His Father, he has no living, saving faith. According to Scripture, here's how we reveal the nature of our faith: "I will show you my faith by what I do" (2:18).

This is why the word *repent* is sometimes used as a synonym for "believe" (Acts 2:38, 3:19, 26:20) and why Mark's one-verse summary of Jesus' preaching is "Repent and believe the good news!" (Mark 1:15). Repenting and believing are two sides of the same coin and must be distinguished but never separated. The word *repent* means to change your mind with the result of change in your life. When by God's Spirit you change your mind about your need for forgiveness and a Savior, you change the direction of your life and come to the Savior.

"Whoever believes in the Son," states the God-inspired promise of John 3:36, "has eternal life." If you believe in the Son, you now have eternal life. You can be sure of it, for Jesus did not die vainly but victoriously, shouting, "It is finished" (John 19:30). This means that He finished the work of saving every person—including you—who believes in Him.

Furthermore, the blood of Christ does not have to be offered for us again. Jesus need not be resacrificed in any manner. We can be sure that by dying once, Jesus Christ did for us what we could never do for ourselves in a thousand lifetimes (Hebrews 9:25-28, 1 Peter 3:18). Enjoy the assurance that God has settled your account forever because He is satisfied with the work of Christ for His people.

**Assurance of Salvation Rests on the Truth of God's Promises**
Because God's promises are true, believers can be assured of salvation.

Our assurance does not rest on the words of a man or woman, no matter how holy we might think that person is. It doesn't depend on the words of the church. Our assurance rests on the firm foundation of the words of God Himself. As the monumental theologian/reformer John Calvin said, "It is the word of God alone which can first and effectually cheer the heart of the sinner. There is no true or solid peace to be enjoyed in the world except in the way of reposing upon the promises of God." [1]

Consider some of the promises of God regarding salvation. His promises are perpetually fresh. So, even if you are familiar with them, try to read them as if for the very first time.

  ◆ "For God so loved the world that he gave his one and only Son, that whoever believes in him shall not perish but have eternal life." (John 3:16)
  ◆ "I tell you the truth, whoever hears my word and believes him who sent me has eternal life and will not be condemned; he

has crossed over from death to life." (John 5:24)
- ◆ "Everyone who calls on the name of the Lord will be saved." (Acts 2:21)
- ◆ "Believe in the Lord Jesus, and you will be saved." (Acts 16:31)

Now think, why has God inspired, written, and preserved these things for us? John tells us: "These are written that you may believe that Jesus is the Christ, the Son of God, and that by believing you may have life in his name" (John 20:31). Do you, because of what is written in the Word of God, "believe that Jesus is the Christ, the Son of God," with all that is implied by those titles? If so, then you may be sure that you "have life in his name" at this very moment.

That's God's intention. He expressly purposes that His great and precious promises lead us to confidently believe that we can participate in an eternal relationship with Him. "He has given us his very great and precious promises," wrote the Apostle Peter, "so that through them you may participate in the divine nature" (2 Peter 1:4). If you believe His promises, your salvation is now and forever definite, for God's Word is true and God is true to His Word.

In His promises, *God Himself assures us* of acceptance. He had these guarantees written so that they would be clear and unmistakable. Another reason He had them recorded is so that every believer at all times and in all places might have the same access to assurance. Although you and I come two thousand years after the first Christians, we may read the same promises given to them for assurance. And regardless of whether we "feel saved" at any given moment, despite our present circumstances or physical condition, God's promises and our condition remain firm and irreversible. So when we read "God has given us eternal life, and this life is in his Son. He who has the Son has life; he who does not have the Son of God does not have life" (1 John 5:11-12), we may take this promise as *direct assurance* for ourselves, if through faith we have the Son.

If you trust the promises of Scripture for your information about salvation, trust them also for your assurance of that salvation. "The Bible is sent," explains Spurgeon, "that you may have full assurance of your possession of eternal life; do not, therefore, dream that it will be presumptuous on your part to aspire to it."[2] Have you believed God's promises from the heart? Then you are entitled to the assurance that you are His child.

## MORE APPLICATION

*Where are you looking for assurance of salvation?* The first place to look for such assurance is Godward, not selfward. Assertions about assurance that begin with "Because I . . ." have their place (as we will see in the next two chapters), but they aren't the starting place.

Assurance of a relationship with God should never be based upon an experience, a ceremony, the opinion of others, or something you have done. Reliance upon these things usually breeds doubt. You wonder if you have had the genuine experience, received from the ceremony what you should have, talked to the right people, or done quite enough. Faith in what God has done, however, produces assurance that's steadier and sturdier.

An introspective young woman told me she had been riding a roller coaster of assurance. Lately she had been in a twisted valley of doubt, clouded by fears that she had deceived herself about her motives, responses, etc., three years earlier when she professed faith in Christ. She had repeatedly asked herself whether "back then" she had "repented right" and "believed right." Recalling this pattern in previous conversations with her, it occurred to me that despite her apparent concern to respond appropriately to the gospel, her focus was misplaced. She was trying to find assurance in what she had done rather than in what God had done. As she has become more Godward in her focus, she has had more consistent assurance and joy in her salvation.

Where are *you* looking for assurance?

*Do you rely on the character of God, trust in the work of Jesus Christ, and believe the promises given by the Spirit of*

*God?* These are the unshakable foundations for the assurance of salvation. All other evidence that leads you to be sure of your salvation should be secondary to and built upon these objective, God-centered facts.

I suppose it's just human nature, though, to want to base our assurance on personal experience, as we do in most things. For instance, the weather forecaster may predict rain, but we feel more certain about it when we see the dark, overcast skies for ourselves. But this tempting tendency can be ruinous when it comes to seeking the assurance of our salvation.

For eighteen years in the early twentieth century, H. A. Ironside was pastor of Moody Memorial Church in Chicago. An elderly man confessed to him desperate struggles with the assurance of his salvation. He told Pastor Ironside how he longed for some definite witness that he could not mistake.

"Suppose," said Ironside, "that you had a vision of an angel who told you your sins were forgiven. Would that be enough to rest on?"

"Yes," the man replied, "I think it would. An angel should be right."

"But," inquired Ironside, "suppose on your deathbed Satan came and said, 'I was that angel, transformed to deceive you.' What would you say?"

The man was speechless.

The pastor told him that God has given us something more reliable and authoritative than the voice of an angel. He has given us His Son and His Word.

Then Ironside asked a question each of us needs to answer: "Isn't that enough to rest on?"[3]

NOTES

1. John Calvin, as quoted in *Calvin's Wisdom: An Anthology Arranged Alphabetically*, comp. Graham Miller (Edinburgh: The Banner of Truth Trust, 1992), page 10.
2. C. H. Spurgeon, "The Blessing of Full Assurance," *Metropolitan Tabernacle Pulpit*, vol. 34 (London: Passmore and Alabaster, 1889; reprint, Pasadena, TX: Pilgrim Publications, 1974), page 273.
3. H. A. Ironside, as quoted in "Take My Word For It!" *Our Daily Bread*, October 8, 1985.

# FOUR

# AN INNER CONFIRMATION

—————— ✞ ——————

*At every point in true assurance, the activity
of the Spirit is essential.*
JOEL BEEKE
*Assurance of Faith*

"Do you think I'm a Christian?" I've been asked that because
I'm a pastor. Some will ask this question of a religious
leader, Bible expert, or another they perceive to be close to God
hoping to be given assurance of a relationship with God. They
think a pronouncement from someone in the ministry is virtually
tantamount to assurance from God Himself.

I have always resisted giving a direct answer to that question. Even if thoroughly convinced that the inquirer is a genuine
Christian, I don't want to usurp the authority of the only One
who can see into that person's heart and has the right to declare
that person His child.

I may tell them, "The Bible says if you've repented and
believed in Christ you are a Christian," or "Here are the biblical
marks of a Christian and they appear to be in your life." However,
I cannot unequivocally say, "Yes, you are a Christian," because I
may be mistaken. If the other eleven disciples did not know Judas
wasn't for real, then we, too, can be in error when evaluating the
presence of faith of others. God alone knows the true condition of
a person's soul.

So it's always best to point people—regardless of age or
intimacy with you—back *to God* whenever they question their
relationship *with God*. He is willing and able to confirm to each
of His children that he or she is His child.

That's why we read in Romans 8:16 that "the Spirit himself testifies with our spirit that we are God's children."

## ASSURANCE MAY BE EXPERIENCED PARTLY THROUGH THE INNER CONFIRMATION OF THE HOLY SPIRIT

If you are a Christian, do you realize that another Person lives with you inside your body? That Person is none other than "the Spirit himself," the Holy Spirit of God, who indwells every believer in Christ (1 Corinthians 6:19). Although indissolubly united, each of you remains a distinct individual. Notice how both are mentioned in Romans 8:16—"*The Spirit himself* testifies with *our spirit*" (emphasis added). Each spirit also communicates to our consciousness. We speak to ourselves, but the Spirit of God communicates to us also. Part of the Spirit's ministry is to communicate to believers an assurance that "we are God's children."

As we have already seen, the Spirit's assuring testimony does not exclude the possibility of a real Christian doubting that he or she is a child of God. But He is the One who helps believers dissolve those doubts. He can convince even the most wicked sinners that God has chosen them to be an object of His everlasting love. He can persuade them to believe that Heaven and the forgiveness of sins are theirs because of the death of Jesus Christ two thousand years ago. The Spirit causes believers to grow in the awareness that they are unworthy of acceptance by God and yet simultaneously forges a faith that leads them to "draw near to God with a sincere heart in full assurance" (Hebrews 10:22).

## HOW DOES THE HOLY SPIRIT GIVE CHRISTIANS THIS ASSURANCE?

Bible-believing scholars disagree over exactly what Romans 8:16 teaches about the process of the Spirit's testimony. Linguistic and theological concerns prompt them to ask, "Does He testify *with* our spirit (as in the translation above) or *to* our spirit?" In other words, does the Holy Spirit work *with* our spirit, influencing our thinking and leading us to decide that we really are saved, but without putting specific words into our heads? Or does He also testify directly *to* our spirit with definite words we hear in our thoughts and with impressions we feel, both of which assure us that "we are God's children"? To think of it still another way, does God's Spirit indirectly testify to us about our salvation by *guiding* the thoughts and impressions we generate ourselves, or does He *give* thoughts and impressions of assurance to us directly? I believe He does both, in whatever balance He deems best.

In one sense, of course, the work of God's Spirit is inscrutable. But even though we can't *fully* explain or describe how He testifies with or to our spirit that we are children of God doesn't mean we can't characterize it at all.

### He Opens Our Minds to Understand the Bible in Ways That Give Us Assurance

No one can rightly understand the Scripture unless the Spirit of God gives that person understanding. First Corinthians 2:14 declares, "The man without the Spirit does not accept the things that come from the Spirit of God, for they are foolishness to him, and he cannot understand them, because they are spiritually discerned." But even the person who has been given the Spirit doesn't immediately understand everything he or she will eventually understand about the Word. Throughout our lives God's Spirit will illumine our minds to understand the Bible.

The testimony of the Spirit with our spirit is His coming alongside us giving new understanding of something in Scripture so that we're more sure of our salvation. Have you ever been reading God's Word or hearing it preached when you suddenly had a flash of insight? Did this insight draw out your heart in love to God, or cause you to thank Him for saving you, or open new vistas into the meaning and application of the Cross? That was the Holy Spirit testifying with your spirit.

The Spirit is the Clarifier of the meaning of God's message to God's children. Whenever you see the truth about your relationship with God as never before, as though a light has come on or something has "clicked," that's the Holy Spirit working in your mind. When God's message seems eminently logical where it had previously seemed confusing, the Holy Spirit is testifying with your spirit. As the uniqueness and glory of Christ in the gospel are increasingly unveiled to you, the Illuminator is active within you. When your objections and rationalizations against assurance are dislodged by the Word of God, it's because the Spirit is applying the force. If you develop an unquenchable desire to know the reality of Christ and the assurance spoken of in Scripture, that's happening because the Assurer is kindling the fire.

This reemphasizes the importance of looking for assurance of salvation in the Book that tells us about salvation. For although "the Spirit himself testifies with our spirit that we are God's children," His testimony is heard primarily through the Book He inspired.

### He Guides Our Thinking About the Biblical Marks of Salvation in Our Lives

The Spirit testifies, or "bears witness" (KJV, NASB), with our spirit when He causes us to discover the biblical marks of a Christian in ourselves. To borrow Paul's words, such assurance is the result of looking for signs of salvation in my life and then "my conscience bearing me witness in the Holy Spirit" that I am saved (Romans 9:1, NASB).

The Holy Spirit is the One who convinces us that we are Christians, but He often does so by guiding our own rational and logical processes in properly evaluating the evidence that He has changed our lives in accordance with His Word. And His testimony does not merely lead us to cold calculations about our salvation, He also ignites joy and comfort from them.

For example, one evidence of salvation is a love for God that draws us to Him and calls out to Him. That's described in the previous verse, Romans 8:15—"You received the Spirit of sonship. And by him we cry, 'Abba, Father.'" The Spirit is giving assurance to Christians when they read this and think, *That's how it is in* my *spirit. I am drawn to God as my heavenly Father and I talk to Him as my Abba (Daddy), not my Judge.* When you truly think God is your *Father*, and prove this by crying to Him as *Father* from your heart, you are *necessarily* implying that you believe you are His *child*. And while it is *your* spirit crying out to your Father, it is "by him" (the Holy Spirit) that you make this cry, thus He is testifying with your spirit that you are God's child.

Another confirmation of true faith is conscious obedience to the Word of God. "We know," states 1 John 2:3, "that we have come to know him if we obey his commands." As I think about my life and examine my heart, I can honestly say that I want to do all that God wills. I do not always obey Him, but the general orientation of my life is decidedly toward obedience rather than disobedience. These thoughts are the result of my own observations and evaluations. But such thinking is not entirely my own. The Holy Spirit influences my thinking so that I come to these conclusions and say these things to myself, thus He testifies *with* my spirit. "Without the Spirit's aid," writes theologian J. I. Packer, "man can never recognize the Spirit's handiwork in himself."[1]

Of course, it is possible to deceive myself, especially when dealing with just one or two biblical evidences of faith. But the Spirit helps me see them on balance with others. Because of Him I realize that I must measure myself against the other marks of a Christian, but also because of Him I *want* to! As I consider other tokens of true conversion, He subconsciously leads me to conclude, "Yes, in all humility I really do think that is true of me; and so is that, and that." Even though self-deception is possible, He warns me of that possibility. Unlike the falsely assured, the Spirit gives God's children a healthy fear of being self-deceived and a constant willingness to examine themselves to insure against it.

### He Brings Scripture and Its Truths to Our Minds
### in Various Ways that Assure Us
Here we begin to speak of the Spirit testifying more *to*, rather than *with*, our spirit. One way He often does this is by bringing the words of familiar Bible verses into the mind for the purpose of strengthening assurance.

On a recent Sunday I was very discouraged. Church attendance was unusually low. I had no sense of God's blessing on my preaching. Although a young woman wanted to chat with my wife over a snack, no one expressed a desire for after-church fellowship with me in the evening as they usually do. Feeling fruitless and ineffective for God's Kingdom, I went home by myself. A half hour of daylight remained, so I jumped on my bike for some sunset cycling and thinking. As I idled along, the breeze on my face brought the laughter of family gatherings and the smells of hamburgers grilling as twilight closed that warm holiday weekend. Everyone seemed to have more blessings than I did. Every home was a mansion to the eyes of this nonhomeowner. In my loneliness it sounded as though everybody else had family near enough to visit. Wrongly, I began to feel unloved by the Lord. I asked Him why even most of His enemies were allowed to own a home, but not I. "Why," I complained, "must I be so far away from my family?" Instantly this verse sprang into my mind like bread out of a toaster: "Everyone who has left houses or brothers or sisters or father or mother or children or fields for my sake will receive a hundred times as much and will inherit eternal life" (Matthew 19:29).

Autosuggestion? I don't think so. My spirit was going in one (downward and sinful) direction, and this verse immediately swiveled my thinking 180 degrees. A knowing smile turned up the left half of my mouth and I said, "You're right, Lord. I am Your servant and have eternal life, and that's better than what anyone else has. Besides, You've promised me a hundred times as much as I've wanted and, unlike these homes and families, Your reward will last forever." His Spirit was testifying to my spirit that I am a child of God.

For many reasons we may expect the Spirit to speak to us through the recognized words of Scripture far more often than any other way. But even when we "hear" verses from the Bible in our mind, there is potential danger. We know from the temptation of Jesus (Matthew 4:1-11, Luke 4:1-13) that Satan may also suggest Scripture for his purposes. How do we defend ourselves against this scheme? The safest way is the method of Jesus: Learn the Bible so well that you'll know when a verse that's come to your attention is out of context or doesn't apply.

Sometimes the Spirit witnesses to our spirit by placing into our thoughts a scriptural truth that has been expressed to us in a sentence from a sermon, the counsel of a friend, a thought from a book, or even an observation in nature. For example, when you see a hen with her chicks or a cat with her kittens, the Spirit may remind you of the Bible's promises of God's love for you.

I believe the Spirit brings words of assurance other than the specific words of Scripture to our minds, but everything He says to us expresses and supports the truth of Scripture. By this means of illumination and application of God's Word, He imparts individual assurance and comfort.

### He Causes an Inner Sense of Assurance Without Words

This is the most mysterious and personalized way the Spirit testifies assurance to the spirit of a child of God. When He chooses to minister like this, He creates an inner sense of assurance without any awareness on your part of words from Him. Receiving assurance in this form occurs at the level of (biblically valid) feelings, impressions, and inward experiences.

Right from the start we must be careful of two extremes. On the left we must not elevate our experiences to the level of Scripture. Experiences, no matter how deep, dramatic, or rapturous, prove nothing in and of themselves. That's why we must distinguish between the *basis* of assurance and the *experience* of assurance. God-given impressions of assurance are delightful blessings and desirable, but our assurance must always rest primarily on the character of God, the work of Jesus Christ, and the truth of God's promises. Without consciously resting on this basis, an experience of assurance is worthless. Spirit-given impressions firmly planted in this solid ground, however, can yield life's richest and most joyful moments. Yet as wonderful as they can be, they are not a constant feeling. If we rely too heavily on *feeling* the love of God, we can become dangerously dependent on this otherwise-blessed spiritual high. In between these experiences we will have little or no assurance. We'll also become more susceptible to false teaching and to counterfeit experiences regarding the Holy Spirit.

The extreme to avoid on the right is a stiff, frigid denial of ever feeling the assuring presence of the Holy Spirit. Surely the Spirit-produced cry of "*Abba*, Father" in Romans 8:15 does not typically come from a dry heart devoid of experience, although it sometimes might. While it's true that the contemporary Church is largely experience-seeking and anti-intellectual, we must not overreact to these tendencies by rejecting the possibility of the Spirit ever causing us to feel sure that we're saved.

Pastor and Bible commentator James Montgomery Boice walks the path between these two extremes when he says,

> I am convinced [Romans 8:16] teaches that there is such a thing as a direct witness of the Holy Spirit to believers that they are sons or daughters of God, even apart from the other "proofs" I have mentioned. In other words, it is possible to have a genuine *experience* of the Holy Spirit in one's heart. Experience the Spirit? I know the objections. I know that no spiritual experience is ever necessarily valid in itself. Any such experience can be counterfeited, and the devil's counterfeits can be very good indeed. But the fact that a spiritual experience can be counterfeited does not invalidate all of them. I also know that those who seek experiences of the Holy Spirit frequently run to excess and fall into unbiblical ideas and practices. Every such experience must be tested by Scripture. But in spite of these objections, which are important, I still say that there can be a direct experience of the Spirit that is valid testimony to the fact that one is truly God's child. Haven't you ever had such an experience? An overwhelming sense of God's presence? Or haven't you at some point, perhaps at many points in your life, been aware that God has come upon you in a special way and that there is no doubt whatever that what you are experiencing is from

God? You may have been moved to tears. You may have deeply felt some other sign of God's presence, by which you were certainly moved to a greater and more wonderful love for him.[2]

This "direct experience of the Spirit" assuring us of our relationship with the Father may be strong and intense, stirring our deepest emotions. At other times He comes gently and quietly, ministering peace and tranquility to the soul. Such impressions of assurance may make you feel as though your body can hardly contain the love you want to express to your "Abba," or they may be a sweet sense that your heavenly Father is lavishing His love upon you.

Then there are those unforgettable encounters where the Spirit testifies to your spirit so that you experience *all* these feelings. That's how the leading figure of America's First Great Awakening, pastor and theologian Jonathan Edwards, described the following event in his journal:

Once, as I rode out into the woods for my health, in 1737, having alighted from my horse in a retired place, as my manner commonly has been, to walk for divine contemplation and prayer, I had a view that for me was extraordinary, of the glory of the Son of God, as Mediator between God and man, and His wonderful, great, full, pure and sweet grace and love, and meek and gentle condescension. This grace that appeared so calm and sweet, appeared also great above the heavens. The Person of Christ appeared ineffably excellent with an excellency great enough to swallow up all thought and conception—which continued, as near as I can judge, about an hour; which kept me the greater part of the time in a flood of tears and weeping aloud. I felt an ardency of soul to be, what I know not otherwise how to express, emptied and annihilated; to lie in the dust, and to be full of Christ alone; to love Him with a holy and pure love; to trust in Him; to live upon Him; and to serve and follow Him; and to be perfectly sanctified and made pure with a divine and heavenly purity. I have, several other times, had views very much of the same nature, and which have had the same effects.[3]

Although it's critical to be careful with the text, in a practical sense the most important teaching in Romans 8:16 is that *the Spirit does communicate assurance to us.* So whether the words in our mind that assure us are always our own or sometimes directly from the Spirit, and whether any feelings of assurance are immediately from the Spirit, is not the main point. The point is not so much precisely *how* He gives us assurance but that He *does.* Chapter 9 will present principles on distinguishing the Spirit's assurance from self-assurance.

## MORE APPLICATION

*If you are not aware of experiencing this ongoing work of the Spirit, you may still need the first work of the Spirit.* The first work of the Spirit of God is to convince people of their sin and its implications, and of their need for Christ to save them from the guilt and judgment for those sins. If the testimony of the Spirit described here is not a familiar experience to you; if while reading this chapter you never thought, *I have moments of assurance like that*; then a possible reason you have no *assurance* of salvation is that you still need *salvation.*

John Wesley is remembered today as a devoted Christian and founder of the Methodist church. But in 1736 he was still unconverted when he came to America as a young Anglican missionary and settled in Savannah, Georgia. The day after he arrived he was introduced to a German Moravian pastor, who questioned Wesley about his personal faith.

"Have you the witness within yourself?" he asked the Englishman. "Does the Spirit of God bear witness with your spirit that you are a child of God?"

Wesley was surprised and didn't know how to answer.

"Do you know Jesus Christ?" the Moravian asked.

"I know He is the Savior of the world," Wesley replied after a pause.

"True," the pastor said, "but do you know He has saved you?"

Wesley answered, "I hope He has died to save me."

"Do you know yourself?" the German persisted.

"I do," Wesley replied, but he added in his journal, "I fear they were vain words."[4]

Do *you* have this testimony of the Holy Spirit within yourself? If you sincerely believe you do, it is not presumption, but God-honoring faith, to say "Yes!" If, like Wesley at this point, you have not known His assuring work, don't be afraid to admit it. Don't let your pride keep you from Christ.

*If you think you have received the assurance of the Holy Spirit, confirm it by the fruit of the Holy Spirit (Galatians 5:22-23).* Assurance is experienced only *partly* through the inner assurance of the Holy Spirit, for it may also be experienced by finding the biblical signs of salvation in your life. The Spirit will not testify assurance to your spirit without testifying of His presence by additional means (see Galatians 5:22-23 for these means). So the best way to ensure that your inward sense of assurance is really from the Spirit is to observe the visible marks of His grace in your life.

One of America's keenest theological thinkers was B. B. Warfield. He penned these penetrating words, which emphasize our need to verify our inner perception of assurance:

A man who has none of the marks of a Christian is not entitled to believe himself to be a Christian; only those who are being led by the Spirit of God are children of God. But a man who has all the marks of being a Christian may fall short of his privilege of assurance. It is to such that the witness of the Spirit is superadded, not to take the place of the evidence of "signs," but to enhance their effect and raise it to a higher plane; not to produce an irrational, unjustified conviction, but to produce a higher and more stable conviction than he would be, all unaided, able to draw.[5]

Make sure that your *impressions* of being a Christian are confirmed by *expressions* of being a Christian. God doesn't intend for them to stand alone, but to strengthen each other. (There's more on this in the next chapter.)

*If you long for more of the assurance of the Holy Spirit, pray for it, persevere in obedience, and patiently wait for God's timing.* Have you realized that the *desire* for assurance of salvation usually signals the *presence* of salvation? And even if you do have a flicker of assurance, you will not sin by praying for more. Don't expect it, however, if you are willfully and remorselessly persistent in a particular sin. Assurance of salvation is for those who are trying to live like saved people. Ultimately, of course, you must wait upon the Lord to give you assurance.

Do you think you are a Christian? If you do, is it because someone told you that you were? I hope one Person *does* tell you so! But I hope you don't believe you're a Christian because a minister, parent, or friend told you so, but because the Holy Spirit has testified with and to your spirit that you are a child of God.

NOTES
1. J. I. Packer, *A Quest for Godliness* (Wheaton, IL: Crossway, 1990), page 184.
2. James Montgomery Boice, *Romans*, vol. 2 (Grand Rapids, MI: Baker, 1992), pages 843-844.
3. Iain Murray, *Jonathan Edwards: A New Biography* (Edinburgh: The Banner of Truth Trust, 1987), page 100.
4. Warren W. Wiersbe and Lloyd M. Perry, *Wycliffe Handbook of Preaching and Preachers* (Chicago: Moody, 1984), page 254.
5. B. B. Warfield, *Faith and Life* (1916; reprint, Edinburgh: The Banner of Truth Trust, 1974), page 187.

# FIVE

# SIGNS OF ETERNAL LIFE
✝

*By making us more holy,*
*God makes us more assured.*
J. W. ALEXANDER
*Consolation*

After the Bible, the all-time best-selling book in the English language is John Bunyan's *Pilgrim's Progress*. It was published in 1678 while Bunyan sat in a British jail. He was persecuted because he would not make the compromises of conscience necessary to minister in the state church, and he kept preaching without the license required then by the government.

*Pilgrim's Progress* is an allegory of the Christian life. The main character is named Christian. He leaves his home, the City of Destruction, because he has read a book (symbolizing the Bible) which said that his city would be destroyed. He has a great burden (representing sin) on his back that nothing can remove. While wandering in the fields outside the city he meets a man named Evangelist. This man points him to a distant wicket gate. Passing through it and along the narrow way beyond, he soon comes to a hill with three crosses. A change comes over him at that point, and the burden slides from his back and down into an empty tomb. From this illustration of salvation, Christian proceeds along the Kingshighway to his final destination, the Celestial City. Along the way he encounters characters and circumstances that portray in story form the journey of a Christian through this life and into Heaven.

At the end of the book, Christian and his companion,

Hopeful, cross a river, which is a picture of death. Hopeful finds it very easy, but Christian thinks on the sins of his past and sinks into "great darkness and horror." In this way Bunyan shows that some believers leave the world with great grace and triumph, while other true Christians may suddenly, in their final breaths, struggle with assurance of their salvation.

Just before Christian and Hopeful cross the river, they pass another pilgrim named Ignorance. He limps along badly, and obviously prefers to make his pilgrimage alone rather than with others who profess to be believers. Christian and Hopeful talk with him, but then Ignorance sends them on ahead.

After Christian and Hopeful traverse the river, Bunyan tells of watching them enter the Celestial City. It is one of the most moving descriptions of Heaven ever written.

Strangely, however, he devotes the last paragraph to the other pilgrim, Ignorance. He notes that Ignorance crosses the river without any problem. Instead of walking into the river and eventually finding firm footing within it, Ignorance is ferried across by a man named Vain-hope. By this Bunyan signifies how the unconverted may have an easy passing from this world to the next, confident in what will prove to be a vain hope of entering the Celestial City of Heaven.

When Christian and Hopeful come out of the water, there are "Shining Ones" to meet them, and they help them up the hill into the city. These angels tell the pilgrims of all the glories they will see and be given as rewards. As they approach, other Shining Ones and many other believers—including loved ones and famous Christians of the past—come out to welcome them. The King commands that the gates be opened to receive them, and they enter into the joy of their Lord amid the shouts of praise to His name.

But no one is there to greet Ignorance. With difficulty he makes his way up the hill alone. As he approaches the gates, he expects them to swing open, but nothing happens. So he begins to knock. Someone looks down and asks what he wants. He pleads for admittance, but the gates stay closed against him. The

King commands the two Shining Ones to go out and take Ignorance, bind him hand and foot, and carry him away. They take him through the air to a door in the side of the hill farther down from the Celestial City. Then they open the door and cast him in there. And in the next-to-last sentence of his classic, Bunyan wrote, "Then I saw that there is a way to hell, even from the gates of heaven."

Bunyan's final scene illustrates what Jesus Himself made plain: namely, many who consider themselves pilgrims to God's Celestial City will, to their untimely horror, be arrested abruptly at the portal of Heaven and cast forever into the pit of hell. All through life they'll believe they're truly on the path to Heaven, only to discover at Heaven's door that they relied on a vain hope.

How can we know the truth before it's too late? How can we find out *now* if God will accept us into His Celestial City? As we discussed in chapter 1, the Bible says we *can* be sure now if Heaven's gates will open to us (1 John 5:13). In fact, it commands us to seek such assurance (2 Peter 1:10), and to examine ourselves (2 Corinthians 13:5) for the biblical evidences of salvation until we find them. God *wants* His children to know for sure that they have believed and that they are His forever.

But just as Christian in *Pilgrim's Progress* had doubts at the moment of death about his sins being forgiven, so it is normal for a real Christian to have occasional doubts about salvation. *Persistent* doubts are a source of major concern. And although no doubts should be ignored, *chronic* worries about salvation must be resolved.

And as Bunyan has also shown us in the character Ignorance, it is typical for nonChristians to think they are safe when they are not, and to have a vain hope—a false assurance of salvation.

Where do we turn for assurance? Oddly enough, even though we learn about God and Jesus and salvation in the Bible, Christians are tempted to go to other things for assurance of biblical salvation. They will look to experiences or rituals or parents or pastors for assurance. But the Bible not only tells about salvation, it tells us where to look for assurance of salvation.

The Bible tells us that assurance of salvation rests primarily in the character of God, the work of Jesus Christ, and the truth of God's promises.

Beyond that, Romans 8:16 tells us that assurance of salvation may be experienced partly through the internal work of the Holy Spirit convincing the Christian that he or she is a child of God.

Although this is a biblical and precious experience available to Christians, it is sometimes problematic. That's because, by nature, this type of assurance is inward, subjective, and individual. We can easily deceive ourselves into thinking we have heard the Spirit's voice. And it is also easy for some Christians, such as those of melancholic temperament or who have never had the assurance of much human love, to doubt if they've really heard the voice of the Spirit assuring them of God's love. So Scripture tells us of another source of assurance.

## ASSURANCE MAY BE EXPERIENCED PARTLY THROUGH THE PRESENCE OF THE ATTITUDES AND ACTIONS THE BIBLE SAYS WILL ACCOMPANY SALVATION

If you are concerned about the assurance of your salvation, the book of the Bible you want to read and reread is the first letter of the Apostle John. As we noted earlier, the expressed purpose of this letter is to help believers gain the assurance of salvation. "I write these things," says John, "to you who believe in the name of the Son of God so that you may know that you have eternal life" (1 John 5:13). In 1 John we are told of at least ten attitudes and actions that characterize Christians only. So if you want to know if you are going to Heaven, examine yourself in the light of these evidences of true Christianity.

### Do You Share the Intimacies of the Christian Life with Other Believers?

That comes from 1 John 1:6-7, "If we claim to have fellowship with him yet walk in the darkness, we lie and do not live by the truth. But if we walk in the light, as he is in the light, we have fellowship with one another, and the blood of Jesus, his Son, purifies us from all sin." Notice particularly verse 7. It says two things are true of us if we walk with God in the light. The second one is that we are forgiven of our sins. But before that it says, "we have fellowship with one another." One mark of people who walk with God and are forgiven is that they have fellowship with other Christians.

The word *fellowship* comes from the Greek word *koinonia*. It means "to share together with." For the follower of Christ it means to talk about and live the Christian life with other Christians. That includes discussing and participating together in even the intimacies of Christian living, such as praying, studying the Bible, ministering, and especially talking about the spiritual life. It involves verbalizing spiritual victories and failures, Scriptural insights, and asking questions of each other's walk with God.

Does this describe you? If you love exchanging insights about the Bible and Christian living, if you hunger to learn from other believers so you can grow in grace and get closer to Christ and live more in obedience to Him, then you are a believer.

NonChristians certainly aren't like this. They emphasize how their faith is a private thing. They believe one's relationship to God is too personal a matter to discuss openly. They'd much rather talk about work, sports, their children, or their hobby than about Christian living or how the Bible relates to these things.

### Do You Have a Deep Awareness of Your Sin Against the Word and Love of God?

I take that from 1 John 1:8,10—"If we claim to be without sin, we deceive ourselves and the truth is not in us. . . . If we claim we have not sinned, we make him out to be a liar and his word has no place in our lives."

Everyone will admit to not being perfect, but that's not what these verses mean. This involves more than just a willingness on occasion to admit that we have been wrong. Growing Christians are scarcely able to do or think anything without seeing their sin in it. They know that if sin were blue, everything they said, did, or thought would be at least some shade of blue.

They recognize the selfishness in their heart even when they do the best and most benevolent of deeds. They know the sinfulness of their thought life right in the midst of some of their most Christlike actions. They are aware of the darkness of the sin inside them when outwardly they model goodness and light. They know that even when they are closest to Christ and most like Christ that sin is still splattered over them like mud.

Christians feel this way because God's Spirit is living inside them. The revealing Spirit progressively illumines God's pure Law to them, and they increasingly see their inconsistency in keeping it. The convicting Spirit shows them that their sin is more than just human failure: It is sin against the Word and the love of God. The glorifying Spirit gradually draws the veil on the character of a Holy God to them, and they discover just how far short of God's glory they are.

Richard Baxter, another English Puritan and contemporary of John Bunyan, wrote a famous and still-printed book about Heaven and being sure of getting there called *The Saints' Everlasting Rest*. In it he said this about the awareness of sin as a sign of salvation: "I think, if I could stand and mention all the other marks of grace, . . . it would appear that the life and truth of all of them lieth in this one."[1] Does the Spirit of God make you aware that your sin violates God's revealed Word? When you sin, do you feel like children who grieve, not because they've done wrong and may be disciplined, but because they feel like they disappointed their Father? If so, then you are a Christian. Strange as it seems, those who feel sin most deeply are those who feel most forgiven (see Luke 7:36-50, especially verse 47; 1 Timothy 1:13-15).

## Do You Live in Conscious Obedience to the Word of God?

This evidence of salvation is found frequently in 1 John, but most clearly in 2:3-5—"We know that we have come to know him if we obey his commands. The man who says, 'I know him,' but does not do what he commands is a liar, and the truth is not in him. But if anyone obeys his word, God's love is truly made complete in him."

A woman told me a relative of hers had died. I asked if he was a Christian. She said, "Oh, yes, he made a profession of faith and was baptized at age seven. He never went back to church or read the Bible in the seventy years after that, but I'm sure he was a Christian." Such a claim is astonishing in light of the statements in these verses. We "know him *if* we obey his commands." No one but Jesus has ever perfectly and consistently obeyed the commands of God; nevertheless, obedience to the Word of God characterizes the lifestyle of a disciple of Jesus. And anyone who "does not do what he commands is a liar" about being born again.

Just as coming to Christ is done consciously, so is living daily in obedience to God's Word. What the Apostle John refers to in this passage does not happen accidentally or unintentionally. Those who know Christ aren't aimless, they obey Him *purposefully*. They become learners of His Word and set out to obey it. Despite frequent failures, they persevere.

I often hear new and growing believers talk about obeying God. Sometimes they'll say how they've come to realize that something they've done (or not done) for a long time was disobedient to God's Word, but now they are consciously obeying. Or they'll say how much they want to obey God's will in a situation but aren't sure yet what it is. Concern for obedience to God is clearly Christian; carelessness is not.

Do you seek out the Word of God, and do you find yourself compelled to obey it? Do you consciously and intentionally try to live out what you encounter in the Bible? Then in the words of 1 John, know that you have come to know God.

**Do You Despise the World and Its Ways?**
Notice 1 John 2:15—"Do not love the world or anything in the world. If anyone loves the world, the love of the Father is not in him."

When this verse speaks of "the world," it's speaking of the

world system, not God's creation. It refers to the world without God, the ungodly ways and things that characterize the world.

Unbelievers love the world and plunge into it because it's all they have. And the more they realize they won't be here forever, the more they immerse themselves into the world to find meaning, hope, pleasure, and satisfaction. They discover, of course, that the world can't fill the hole in their heart, but they keep trying because they don't have anything else (unless they come to Christ).

Despite their endless dissatisfaction, worldly people (that is, nonChristians) do love the world. Their greatest loves are in things where God is not central. These things may be cultured and refined, or they may be lewd and base, but they are pursued without thoughts of God. NonChristians will love sports, sex, money, property, work, travel, retirement, children, hobbies, television, learning, computers, art, grandchildren, collecting, reading, music, shopping, or any number of things more than God. The world finds the church and the things of God the most boring things imaginable. At best it finds them much less meaningful than other things. And the people of the world can't understand why we don't get as excited as they do about the things that turn them on (see also 1 Peter 4:3-4).

Christians, however, feel less at home in this world the more they grow spiritually. They also look increasingly toward their true and eternal home, the Celestial City.

### Do You Long for the Return of Jesus Christ and to Be Made Like Him?

John speaks of the second coming of Jesus in 1 John 3:2-3—"Dear friends, now we are children of God, and what we will be has not yet been made known. But we know that when he appears, we shall be like him, for we shall see him as he is. Everyone who has this hope in him purifies himself, just as he is pure."

The Christian can hardly wait for Jesus to fulfill His promise to return to the earth (Matthew 24, 26:64; John 14:3). The one who knows Christ often thinks, *I wish He would come today.* Trying to imagine the glorious place where he or she will spend eternity, the Christian daydreams about what life will be like in "a new heaven and a new earth" where Jesus reigns (Revelation 21:1). Like a bride anticipating her wedding day, so those who are part of the bride of Christ—the Church—expectantly await their union with Jesus at His return.

Part of the believer's expectancy about seeing Christ is in becoming "like him." At that moment, the Bible says "we will all be changed—in a flash, in the twinkling of an eye" (1 Corinthians 15:51-52). The same chapter talks about the splendor, glory, power, and immortality of the new "spiritual body" to be given to God's children. With it will come the complete and final deliverance from sin's presence that the Christian groans for.

The result of anticipating the return of Jesus, according to 1 John 3:3, is that the believer "purifies himself, just as he [Christ] is pure." I remember hearing as a child that I shouldn't do anything I would be ashamed of if Jesus returned and found me doing it. Such talk must sound old-fashioned today, for I haven't heard it in years. And of course, the Lord knows now, not just at His return, when we do something wrong. Still, this attitude should represent the heart of a Christian, young or old.

Do you sometimes look at the clouds and visualize Jesus' triumphant arrival? Have you mused about looking into His radiant face and being transformed? Do you ever longingly wonder what it will be like never to think another sinful thought or commit another sinful act? If you do, take heart, for unbelievers don't often or seriously think of these things. These things *are* the Christian's dreams.

### Do You Habitually Do What Is Right More and Sin Less?
John wrote plainly in 1 John 3:7-8,10:

> Dear children, do not let anyone lead you astray. He who does what is right is righteous, just as he is righteous. He who does what is sinful is of the devil, because the devil has been sinning from the beginning. . . . This is how we know who the children of God are and who the children of the

devil are: Anyone who does not do what is right is not a child of God; neither is anyone who does not love his brother.

All people do some things they would consider righteous and some things they wouldn't. So it's easy for most people to believe they are righteous because they do some things that appear righteous. But much of the meaning of these verses turns on the word *does*. Each time it's used here it's in the present tense, referring to patterns and habitual action. So when it says "He who does what is right is righteous," it doesn't say the Christian can never commit acts of sin. Instead it means that a Christian is one who, throughout his or her life, habitually does what is right more and sins less.

This life change is not found merely in the power of the Christian's own resolve, but because of the work of Christ for him or her and the power of the Holy Spirit within him or her. "For we know that our old self was crucified with him," wrote the Apostle Paul in Romans 6:6, "so that the body of sin might be done away with, that we should no longer be slaves to sin." When a person is born again, that person is instantly forgiven of the guilt of sin, and the enslaving power of sin is broken so that it gradually loses its grip over his or her life. Complete liberation from the presence of sin doesn't occur until death (or the Lord's return, whichever is first), but an overall tendency toward obedience is present now for the child of God.

Pastor and author John MacArthur explains the difference between the Christian who "does what is right" but sins frequently and the nonChristian whose life is a pattern of sin:

> I frequently receive letters from anguished Christians who doubt their salvation because they can't seem to break a sinful or unwise habit. They most often write about smoking, overeating, and masturbation. They fear their struggle with such things means they are locked into a pattern of sin. But John is not saying that the frequent occurrence of one particular sin in a person's life means that person is lost. . . .

A person who rejects God's authority doesn't care what God thinks about his habits, and is obviously not a Christian. A Christian, however, has a drastically different way of relating to God ... A true Christian can still sin, and may even do so frequently, but *sinning frequently* is not the same as *practicing sin*. In 1 John we see that a true believer can do the first, but not the second.[2]

If you hope you are a Christian, look at your life this way: Over the past few years, has it been your habit to do what is right more and more, and to sin less? Can you point to specific things and say, "I believe I am living by God's Word more than I was some time ago; I know I customarily do more of what I know God says is right than I used to. And I think that overall, the habits of my life are less sinful than they used to be"?

Notice that the emphasis in these verses isn't on what a Christian *doesn't* do, but on what he *does*. Some people, as we said before, feel spiritually secure primarily because of the things they do not do. But when the Bible talks about assurance, it emphasizes what's on your "to *do*" list as much as what's on your "*not* to do" list, what's on your list of loves as well as your list of hates.

So, where some would say, "I don't miss church," John would also ask, "But do you habitually seek God in Scripture and prayer privately during the week?" Where some would say, "I don't cheat on my taxes," John would ask, "But does your giving please God?" Where some would say, "I don't break the law," John would ask, "But do you obey what God says about the use of the tongue, about dealing with bitterness, about forgiving others?" Where some would say, "I don't run around on my spouse," John would ask, "But are you a loving husband or wife?" Where some would say, "I don't miss work," John would ask, "But are you faithful in serving God through His church?" Where some would say, "I don't hurt or hate anyone," John would ask, "But whom do you help and love for the sake of Jesus?"

Which of these two types of attitudes describes you? As you look back over the past few years, if you can honestly say that you habitually do what is right more and sin less, then you are most certainly a Christian.

## Do You Love Other Christians Sacrificially and Want to Be with Them?

Few marks of a true believer are as underestimated as the one in 1 John 3:14—"We know that we have passed from death to life, because we love our brothers."

Although it's true that love for *all* people should characterize followers of Jesus, this verse specifically refers to loving "our brothers," that is, other Christians. Surely, no professing Christian would claim to *not* love others in God's family, but the love John requires of believers entails more than that. This love is more than just a fondness or preference, it's a sacrificial love.

At the very least it is a love that makes you want to be with others Christians and willing to sacrifice to do so. Do you have that kind of love? If you do, you'll want to be with the children of God when they are together to worship their Father, to talk to Him, and to learn what He has said.

To "love our brothers" is much more than this, but it is at least this. When we have Christ's love for each other we meet needs in the family, we help those who hurt or are weak, we "rejoice with those who rejoice; mourn with those who mourn" (Romans 12:15), etc. Behind all this Christian family love is the sacrifice of our time, starting with the time required to gather when the family gathers.

Many have been deluded about whether they love the people of God. They think they love them when they don't, and they prove they don't by relinquishing little or nothing for them. Their "love" is limited by convenience; the Christian's is liberated by sacrifice.

A member of our church, even in the midst of job stress and moving from one apartment to another, has been showing up unannounced to mow the yard for me on occasion so I would have more time to write this book. This person often gives up privileges and preferences in similar ways for others in the church family, not just for me. That's love.

There are countless ways, of course, to show the love of Christ to your brothers and sisters in Christ. Even giving financially can be a way to express love to believers in other lands. But followers of Jesus *will sacrifice*, even profits and pleasures if necessary, because of the depth of their love for their family and Father. Do you do this?

**Do You Discern the Presence of the Holy Spirit Within You?**
Observe what John wrote in the last half of 1 John 3:24 and in 4:13—"This is how we know that he lives in us: We know it by the Spirit he gave us. . . . We know that we live in him and he in us, because he has given us of his Spirit."

This is very much like Romans 8:16. But even those who have difficulty discerning the testimony of the Spirit within them should be able to discern the fruit of the Spirit's presence within them. Just as sap rises within a tree and eventually, but surely, produces fruit, so God's Spirit within a person produces fruit.

Paul listed several qualities in Galatians 5:22-23, which he called the fruit of the Spirit. We've talked about the first on the list—love—so let's consider the next one, joy. Are you aware of a joy in God? This is a fair question for all professing Christians, even children and teenagers. I see many people who claim to be Christians give the impression that they never have moments of sheer joy in knowing God. But if you have occasions, such as in public or private worship, times when you are thrilled with God because He is God, or just because you are His—that is excellent evidence that you know God. Anyone who truly knows the infinite and Holy Triune God cannot help but have moments where he or she finds sheer delight in Him.

The Holy Spirit of Almighty God cannot live in a human being without making Himself known. Whenever there is a human spirit in a body, that spirit makes itself known. It moves the body, it communicates through the body, it gives evidence that there is life within that body. When the Holy Spirit is in someone's body, He will make Himself known also. Whether it is speaking assurance in the person's mind, or causing the person to love God or hate the world, or to look forward to Christ's return, or to sacrificially love other Christians, or to become overjoyed sometimes just in thoughts of God, the Spirit will give evidence—fruit—of His presence. And the Christian should be able to observe some of this fruit and say, "The only explanation for this is the Spirit's presence, and that means that I am a child of God."

## Do You Enjoy Listening to the Doctrines the Apostles of Jesus Taught?

This is the proof of faith given in 1 John 4:6—"We are from God, and whoever knows God listens to us; but whoever is not from God does not listen to us. This is how we recognize the Spirit of truth and the spirit of falsehood."

John could say without arrogance and as a matter of fact that he and the other apostles of Jesus were from God. There was clear evidence of that. Therefore, he knew that those who knew God would listen to him and the other apostles, and those who were not from God would not listen.

The apostles were all dead by about AD 100, John being the last of them. So here's how we apply this test of a Christian today: Do you enjoy listening to the doctrines the apostles of Jesus taught? If you do, this probably means you are a Christian. I say "probably" because there are some who take a mere academic and philosophical interest in apostolic doctrine. But if you *love their teachings from the heart* and *listen to them so you can obey them*, you are a Christian. And if you don't care to listen to these things, that shows that you are not a real believer.

After the Day of Pentecost, notice what was first on the list of the activities and cravings of these new Christians: "They devoted themselves to the apostles' teaching" (Acts 2:42). Just as a baby is born with the desire to eat, so every person born spiritually has a natural hunger for "every word that comes from the mouth of God" (Matthew 4:4).

Do you desire more than just "how to" kinds of Scripture

studies? Do you find that sermons which are little more than long strings of stories fail to feed your soul after a while? Are you hungry to hear the Bible taught in depth? Do you love to discuss the Bible at length with other Christians? These are good signs. Unbelievers rarely have anything that even comes close to desires like these.

**Do You Believe What the Bible Teaches About Jesus Christ?**
Notice the first half of 1 John 5:1—"Everyone who believes that Jesus is the Christ is born of God."

The Old Testament told of a *Messiah* (the Old Testament word for "Christ") who was to come. The New Testament tells us that Jesus Christ is that Messiah, that Anointed One of God (Mark 8:29; John 1:41, 4:25-26; Romans 9:5). Jesus was the One (and only One) sent by the Father to do all that was needed to bring His people to Himself. All that Jesus spoke and did was in fulfillment of His role as the Christ of God. The Christian is one who believes all that the Scriptures say about Jesus.

The Bible does not ask us for unthinking credulity regarding Jesus Christ. Instead it feeds the mind with nutritious evidence for faith. The greatest evidence of all is His resurrection from the dead. There is not room here to state the many and indomitable arguments supporting Jesus' resurrection. I simply want to note how insurmountable the evidence is. What could God have done to provide a more powerful validation of the claims of Christ? If He had inscribed, "JESUS IS MY SON, BELIEVE IN HIM!" permanently in the sky, people would have still been skeptical and searched for human explanations. If He had written, "JESUS IS GOD!" with the stars of the heavens, it would be dismissed as a Christian conspiracy using lasers, satellites, or another high-tech method, if not sheer coincidence. But to do something as incomparable as raising Jesus from the grave, never to die again, is the perfect foundation for faith. How could God have been more convincing? As a result, we may believe that all the other claims made by and about Jesus will be fulfilled also, including His promise to save and take to Heaven all who believe in Him.

Christians do not believe that Jesus was merely a "great teacher" or an "ascended master." They confess that, just as He claimed, He is "*the* way and *the* truth and *the* life" and that there is no other way to God the Father but through Him (John 14:6, emphasis added). They do not doubt that He is the "King of kings and Lord of lords" (Revelation 19:16).

Whether it is the prophecies about Him given centuries before; or the testimony about His miraculous virgin birth, His sinless life, His miraculous power, His substitutionary death, His bodily resurrection, or His second coming; the Christian believes what the Bible teaches about Jesus.

## MORE APPLICATION

*Do you have the assurance of salvation that comes from the presence of the biblical evidences of salvation?* Christians should examine themselves for all the evidences of salvation mentioned in 1 John. Probably some will be seen more clearly than others. But it is vital to look at this list and compare it with your life. If none of these things are present, your spiritual experiences in the past do not matter; and any voices you think to be from God are a deception.

But if they do describe you, then you are entitled to the unshakable assurance that God is your Father, that Jesus has died for you, that all your sins are forgiven forever, and that you are on your way to the Celestial City.

*Beware of presumption.* As there are warnings regarding the testimony of the Holy Spirit, so there are warnings here. On the left is the ditch of presumption, and into it fall those who fail to examine themselves by these evidences. Because they have been in church for years, or have heard these things before, or consider themselves good people, they overrate their spiritual condition and never *verify* in themselves the presence of these marks of a Christian. If you casually dismiss the role of self-examination and Christian evidences to trust in what you think is the inward testimony of the Holy Spirit, you may be greatly deceived.

This is the most important issue of your existence. Don't take it for granted. "Examine yourselves to see whether you are in the faith; test yourselves" (2 Corinthians 13:5).

***Beware of unreasonable self-condemnation.*** On the right is the ditch of hypercritical self-examination. Simply because you have read this far you're probably more likely to fall into this error than the previous one. Its victims are those who think each of these evidences must be fully mature and always noticeable (which is impossible) before they are entitled to assurance.

Because they aren't *perfectly* obedient to God's Word, *completely* loathing of the world, *infallibly* loving of other Christians, etc., they are reluctant to receive assurance. Like those trying to attain salvation by works, they can always find another rung to climb before they reach the top of the ladder of assurance. No matter what they do, they always look for more to do before they will believe that they are Christians. When they look into the mirror of God's Word, particularly in 1 John, they only look for what is wrong with their evidences rather than what is right. They dwell on what is lacking rather than on what is present.

But the Bible requires only the *presence* of evidences, not the *perfection* of them. The flowers of evidence in the bud are flowers nonetheless. And though they are not fully mature, the desire for them to be so (and the grief that they are not) are blossoms formed only by faith in Christ. The Holy Spirit *first* changes our affections and *then* effects changes in our actions. If your heart is drawn toward the characteristics of Christians we've seen in 1 John and you want to see them formed in you, then believe that God is at work in you.

Concern about your inability to live up to God's standards is also a good sign. Those who don't experience some discouragement about their failures in discipleship are either unconverted or live unexamined lives. In that sense your discouragement itself may be another assuring sign of spiritual life. The renowned Puritan theologian John Owen agreed: "I do not understand how a man can be a true believer in whom sin is not the greatest burden, sorrow and trouble."[3] Let that discouragement also be a reminder that you are not saved by what you are supposed to do but rather by trusting in Christ. There is salvation in one look to Christ, even with the simplest understanding of the gospel, even with the weakest faith. Don't be so stringent and ruthless in your self-examination that you lose sight of the Cross and the power of Jesus to save sinners.

John Bunyan was right, of course. There is a real Celestial City and it's called Heaven. One day you will be standing before it. Imagine for a moment that you are at the gate. It is the most solemn moment of your existence. All preparation for this moment is over. There is no second chance.

As you now imagine standing where one day you really will be standing, as you look intently at the gate, will it open for you? *How* do you know? You *can* know. *Do* you know? If you know it will *not* open for you, you need to repent and believe in the only One who can open the door for you.

If you *hope* it will open for you but *aren't sure*, you need to pray and meditate over the scriptures in this chapter until God makes your spiritual condition known to you.

If you *know* it *will* open for you and you know why, you need to thank and worship God, and to rejoice over the most glorious news in the world, that your name is written in Heaven.

NOTES

1. Richard Baxter, *The Practical Works of Richard Baxter* (1649; reprint, Ligonier, PA: Soli Deo Gloria, 1990), vol. 3, page 204.
2. John MacArthur, Jr., *Saved Without a Doubt* (Wheaton, IL: Victor, 1992), pages 77-78.
3. John Blanchard, comp., *Gathered Gold* (Welwyn, England: Evangelical Press, 1984), page 289.

## SIX
# A SPIRITUAL MIND-SET

———————  ✝  ———————

*Those who are "spiritually-minded" are born of God,*
*. . . and shall come to the enjoyment of him.*
JOHN OWEN
*The Works of John Owen*

"There it goes! Way back! It might be, it could be, it *is!* . . . *A home run! A grand slam!* I can't believe it! This is the *greatest*, most *exciting* finish in World Series *history!*"

I had already thrown my helmet into air, rounded first base, and was leaping like an impala toward second by the time the announcer said, "The Cardinals are world champions!" It was the zenith of baseball drama. Three balls. Two strikes. Two out. Bases loaded. Bottom of the ninth. Last game of the World Series. We're three runs down. I stepped out of the box and did all the things nervous batters do even when it isn't necessary—knocked the dirt out of my spikes, held the bat behind my head with both hands and quickly twisted my torso twice each way, took a practice swing, adjusted my helmet, breathed deeply, made sure the "Louisville Slugger" label faced me, dug back in with my right foot, and tapped the outside corner.

Never had I concentrated so hard, never had I found it so hard to concentrate. "Don't swing at a bad pitch," I said to myself as I riveted my eyes on the horsehide in the pitcher's hand. "But you've got to swing at anything that's close. Whatever you do, *don't strike out!*" Every one of the fifty thousand people in the stadium was standing and screaming. A hundred million people were watching on television. For the rest of their lives, people would remember where they were when they saw the next five seconds. For generations to come, men would tell their children about what I did with this pitch.

In it came. A heater right in my wheelhouse. The swing was pure instinct. A sharp, wooden crack—and my name became a household word.

If you've ever hit a fastball with the sweet spot of a bat, you know how magical the world seems for a moment. And the world never felt more wondrous than at that moment. Before I got to third, fans were spilling over the walls, past the hopelessly outnumbered policemen, and converging on me as if I were giving a million dollars to the first one who reached me. Pushing past them, I finally reached home, leaped on it with both feet and bounced into the waiting mob of teammates. Like a human tsunami, they rushed me with a force that flattened me. After the initial crush, we were up hugging and bouncing like ecstatic three-year-olds. Then I felt something under my legs and before I knew it I was aloft on the shoulders of two fellow players. The crowd roared even louder.

You'd think you'd get used to something like this after you'd been through it a few times, but I never have. I first hit this home run when I was about six, yet it has never lost its thrill for me, even though I've won at least a thousand World Series' championships with a thousand other grand slams.

Of course, I've known similar equally exciting moments. The long, incredible touchdowns I scored to win several Super Bowls were exhilarating. The last-second, seventy-five-foot shots to win NCAA and NBA championships were electrifying also.

What? You've never seen them? Well, I have. Many times.

Each of us daydreams on occasion, as we have since early childhood, about fantasies. Most of us have fantasized about what we'd do if we inherited millions of dollars from some long-lost relative—where we'd live, what kind of home we'd build, what kind of car we'd drive, where we'd travel, etc.

Perhaps you've daydreamed about being a courageous battlefield hero, or a lovely ballerina, or a graceful Olympic figure skater. Some fantasize about life as an accomplished singer or musician, or a master craftsman, or as someone living "happily ever after." Maybe you sometimes imagine how it would be as a spellbinding speaker, a top-gun jet-fighter pilot, or retired to a quiet life in a lakeside cabin, far from crowds and hurry.

Doubtless you've had fantasies of Heaven and what life is like there. And you've probably tried to imagine the horrors of hell. Continuing on the darker side, it's not uncommon to fantasize occasionally, without limitation or accountability, about different physical pleasures.

But of all your fantasies, which is strongest? Which daydream, when you imagine it, thrills you more than any other? In his or her best moments, the Christian would choose to be in Heaven with God and to be made perfect and without sin. Although the Christian daydreams about earthly things, too— even sinful things—the Christian's most consistently absorbing imagination is with spiritual things and the things of God.

But that's not true with others. The nonChristian can identify himself as one who, if he or she could indulge any fantasy, would choose to indulge some sin. The nonChristian's most compelling wish is to gratify a sinful craving without restraint, without law, without limit, and ultimately, without God.

This illustrates the difference between the Christian and the nonChristian described in Romans 8:5—"Those who live according to the sinful nature have their minds set on what that nature desires; but those who live in accordance with the Spirit have their minds set on what the Spirit desires."

This verse recognizes only two kinds of people. "Those who live according to the sinful nature" aren't "less spiritual" Christians than "those who live in accordance with the Spirit." Throughout verses 4-8, there are only two types—those who live by the sinful nature and those who live by God's Spirit, nonChristians and Christians.

Both the King James and the New King James versions of the Bible use a term in verse 6 that is helpful. Instead of referring to "minds set on what the Spirit desires," they speak of being "spiritually minded." This doesn't mean nonChristians who think about the invisible, spiritual realm are spiritually minded. The term still means to have a mind oriented specifically toward the things of *God*. But I want to use the term in this chapter, and let me first use it to ask you, "Are you 'spiritually minded'?" It's a critical question for the following reason.

## ONLY THOSE WHO ARE SPIRITUALLY MINDED ARE CHRISTIANS

These verses teach us that what you set your mind on indicates your spiritual condition. In other words, the thoughts of your mind reveal the state of your soul. If your mind is set on the sinful nature and earthly things instead of on heavenly things, then you are in spiritual death; you are not a Christian.

The Bible speaks of the same thing in Philippians 3:18-19, of "enemies of the cross of Christ. Their destiny is destruction, their god is their stomach, and their glory is in their shame. *Their mind is on earthly things*" (emphasis added).

So each of us belongs to one of two groups of people: nonChristians who set their minds on the sinful nature and things of the world, or Christians who set their minds on the things of the Spirit of God.

Obviously, there are different levels within each group. There are nonChristians who live according to the gross and flagrant desires of the sinful nature. But there are also moral, well-respected people who, despite their morality, do not live according to the Spirit of God.

On the other side, there are Christians who demonstrate in every area of life the priority of following Christ, and there are those usually known as "backslidden." But the backslidden also have their minds set on the things of the Spirit of God because He is in their minds. In the midst of their backslidden condition, they are constantly hounded about their sin by the Spirit of God. Even when choosing to do wrong, they have to do so over the voice of the Spirit, who keeps reminding them about obedience to God, confronting them about the will of God, and urging them back to the ways of God. Though backsliders are long negligent or resistant to the things of the Spirit, their minds are never void of the voice of the Spirit. To some degree then, even those who are backslidden are "spiritually minded" because they "have their minds set on what the Spirit desires." That's why eventually they return to faithfulness.

My wife, Caffy, and I have a close friend who was backslidden for two years. She moved, changed jobs, and was so secretive that we couldn't find her. Reverting to her preconversion days, she twice lived with men for months at a time and frequented bars. Mercifully, God granted her repentance and drew her back to Himself and faithful Christian living. After hearing me express the things in the previous paragraph, she told me, "That's absolutely true. The whole time I was away God was convicting me that I was sinning. I couldn't get Him out of my thoughts. He was always bringing Bible verses to my mind. I kept trying to do what I thought would make me happy, but I was miserable. I was even more miserable than when I did these things before I became a Christian because now the voice of God was in my mind."

How your mind is set refers to what you think about. What your mind is set on is especially revealed in the things you think about when your mind is in neutral, that is, when you daydream, when you aren't forced to think about anything specific. For example, the kinds of things you most often think about when you are driving; when you're about to fall asleep; when you awaken in the night and lie sleepless; when you are gazing out the window of the car, train, or plane; or when you are waiting, say, in line at a store, reflect your mind-set.

What you have your mind set on also refers to the kinds of things you are most interested in, the things that excite you most, the things you feel most deeply about, and the things you enjoy discussing and pursuing more than anything else.

The minds of nonChristians, according to Romans 8:5, are "set on what that [sinful] nature desires." We tend to think only of bodily or sexual sins when we hear about "the sinful nature," but it's much broader than that. In general it means to be consumed with earthly things rather than, by contrast, the things of the Spirit of God.

But even more broadly, to think of *anything* without ever thinking of its relationship to God is to think "according to the sinful nature." That's why people can commonly consider some of the noblest things on earth and still not be "spiritually minded."

To summarize, setting your mind on the things of the sinful nature means that in *whatever* you think about or do, God is not in the center of it. Those who characteristically think like that have not been born into the family of God.

Christians, on the other hand, simply think differently. They are spiritually minded. Spiritual mindedness is an easy and reliable evidence of salvation you can see within yourself. Many nonChristians appear to have some of the outward marks of a Christian. They may be honest with money, love their families, work faithfully, treat people kindly, help others, etc. Despite all these things, they may be Muslims, atheists, Mormons, or simply uninterested in pursuing actively the things of God through the Bible and church. How can you tell if there really is a difference between your soul and theirs? How do you know whether the Holy Spirit lives within you or whether you've deceived yourself? *The* distinguishing mark between true believers who have the Spirit of God and all unregenerate people, according to Romans 8:5, is the set of the mind—what you think about.

My understanding of what this means has been deepened by what an Englishman named John Owen wrote about Romans 8:5 over 300 years ago.[1] He points out the following.

## YOU ARE SPIRITUALLY MINDED WHEN YOU THINK ABOUT THE THINGS OF GOD SPONTANEOUSLY AND WITHOUT EXTERNAL CAUSES

Everyone thinks about God and the things of God sometimes, but it is vital to discover the *source* of those thoughts. Unlike the unconverted, the spiritually minded think about the Lord and spiritual things *spontaneously.*

Jesus said, as recorded in John 4:14, "Whoever drinks the water I give him will never thirst. Indeed, the water I give him will become in him a spring of water welling up to eternal life."

When the Holy Spirit is within you, He causes thoughts of God and spiritual things to spring up within you as spontaneously as an artesian well.

Not long ago I saw a television adaptation of a Sherlock Holmes mystery. In this adventure, a woman had disappeared and a Mr. Green, who loved her, was deeply upset. Holmes believed she had been kidnapped by a known murderer, but didn't know where to find her. As the sleuth contemplated his next move, Green's fears got the best of him.

Holmes said to him, "Calm yourself! Stop thinking of her possible condition."

Green snaped back, "Do you think I *want* to think about it, Mr. Holmes? Such thoughts come *unbidden!*"

His response illustrates what spiritual mindedness means in Romans 8:5. Green thought about her spontaneously because he loved her. His mind was set on her. And we all understand that. We think about what our minds are set on. If your mind is set on your work, you often think about it. If your mind is set on your children, you frequently think about them. And when your mind is "set on what the Spirit desires," you often *spontaneously* think about spiritual things. Even when you aren't trying to meditate on God or the Bible, thoughts related to Him spontaneously come into your mind.

Everyone thinks about God or the things of God sometimes. Unspiritually minded persons hearing the preaching of the Word of God may have thoughts of God, but the source is external. Such thoughts come down like rain upon them, not up like a spring from within them.

Perhaps something on the radio or television puts a thought of God into their heads. Or they may have brief Godward thoughts when a child or friend broaches a question about God or the Bible, or when they see a Christian acting on his or her faith. Such thoughts may be commonplace, but are not spontaneous.

Maybe some calamity or injury or illness or family situation makes them think about God or judgment or eternity. Some need may arise that prompts them to turn to God and pray. But all their thoughts of God are from *external* causes. With a Christian such thoughts come *unbidden*.

Someone may be thinking, "You just don't understand my situation. I'm so busy all day long that I rarely have time to think about God or spiritual things."

That's the point. It doesn't matter how busy you are, a Christian can't help but think of God spontaneously throughout the day. It's not *you* who consciously decides to take your mind off the work before you and focus it on spiritual things (although sometimes that happens). As you don't have to consciously think to breathe, so you don't have to consciously bring up thoughts of God.

## YOU ARE SPIRITUALLY MINDED WHEN YOU
## THINK ABOUT THE THINGS OF GOD
## MORE THAN ANYTHING ELSE

There is no greater evidence of conversion than a change in the whole direction of your thinking. To think wrongly and very little about God and the things of God all your life, and then to begin thinking about spiritual things more than anything else is solid proof of the work of God's grace.

When you are spiritually minded, you not only think of spiritual things spontaneously, but also *abundantly*. Spiritual thoughts abound in the mind of a Christian like leaves on a tree. Compare a tree's leaves to a believer's spiritual thoughts, and its fruit to his or her spiritual deeds. There are always more leaves than fruit. That is not to minimize the importance of spiritual fruit, for fruit is also an indispensable evidence of salvation (see chapter 5). And even though the deeds of spiritual fruit may be more lasting, the leaves of spiritual thoughts are more numerous.

The writer of Psalm 119 testified to his daily abundance of spontaneous spiritual thoughts. In verse 97 he exclaims, "Oh, how I love your law! I meditate on it all day long." That doesn't mean he always had a scroll in his hand. It means he always had the Word of God bubbling up in his mind.

When you are spiritually minded, you think about the things of God more than anything else because you think about almost everything from a spiritual perspective. When you think about your job, you wonder, *If I did things this way, would it be a good witness? . . . Lord, please help me make the right decision. . . . How does the Bible speak to this situation?* Your parental thoughts become Godward thoughts when you're spiritually minded. You're always thinking of how to raise your children Christianly. While disciplining your child you think, *Lord, forgive me if I am doing this in anger. . . . Please help me discipline my child always in a biblical way. . . . Father, I don't want to exasperate my child; I really want to show Your love.*

When you think of money, sports, or even sex, you soon wonder what God's perspective is on the matter, or even what He is thinking about your thoughts at that moment.

Natural disasters prompt you to think of the Judgment. Tramping through the leaves on a glorious fall day causes you to think of the creativity and glory of God. When your breath is taken by a beautiful sunset, you try to imagine Heaven. You can hardly look at billowing clouds in a blue sky without thinking of Christ's return. When you are spiritually minded, everything reminds you of something related to God.

Most conclusive of all, if you are spiritually minded, even when you *sin* you think of God! Sometimes Christians will immerse themselves in thought about sinful things for long periods. The Bible says that while we are in this world, even the best Christians will still think about sinful matters and do sinful deeds. But the Spirit often warns you that what you are thinking or tempted to do is against God and His Word. Frequently your conscience burns *even in the midst of the sinful act* with the awareness that you are breaking the Law of God and displeasing Him. Immediately afterward you know you have grieved the Holy Spirit, and you regret what you've done. Despite your shame, you come to a God whom you know to be holy, confess your sin, and ask His forgiveness.

Why would anyone think of God at the moment he or she is sinning against Him? Why would anyone, with the shame of sin freshly smeared over his or her face, want to turn at once to a

Holy God? It's unnatural! Ah, there's the explanation. Christians do not think "naturally." They think spiritually, they are spiritually minded. And they do so only because the Holy Spirit within them is always pushing thoughts of God to the forefront of their thinking. No matter which way you turn a compass, its needle will soon point northward. Similarly, no matter what a Christian thinks about, his or her mind soon looks Godward. That's spiritual mindedness.

## YOU ARE SPIRITUALLY MINDED WHEN YOU THINK ABOUT THE THINGS OF GOD WITH MORE DELIGHT AND ENJOYMENT THAN ANYTHING ELSE

Scientists say thousands of thoughts flash into our minds daily. Which types do you most love to linger upon? The spiritually minded typically find more joy in thoughts of God and the things of God than anything else.

This doesn't mean Christians shouldn't overflow with love for their children, or feel deeply stirred by a stunning spectacle in nature, or be so excited over a ball game that they yell and jump around. But it does mean there is a quality of delight in God and the things of God that transcends all other things.

With the spiritually minded, there are times of public and private enjoyment of God that overwhelm them with a sense that this was what they were made for. The *Westminster Catechism* opens with this question: "What is the chief end of man?" In other words, "What were we made for?" And the unforgettable answer is, "To love God and to enjoy Him forever." The spiritually minded understand that, for they both love and enjoy God more than anyone or anything else. They know that God is not Someone merely to be obeyed, but to be loved and enjoyed.

Do you *enjoy* thinking about God? Those who are not spiritually minded don't delight in thoughts of God. They can't. Romans 8:7 states that their "sinful mind is hostile to God." They always have one of three options. Either they are so terrified of Him that they can't think of Him; they feel so guilty because of their sin that they can't long think of Him; or they choose the more common response, which is to construct wrong views of Him and believe in a God who conforms to their own desires.

So they invent for themselves a God who is *only* a God of love, who winks at sin and will make exceptions in their case at the Judgment. They can't conceive of a God who created hell. They never think of a God who expects absolute obedience and sacrifice. They never envision God requiring anything of them that they don't want to do. They never consider a God who is at all unpleasant to their way of thinking or living. They would have God be anything but what He really is and reveals Himself fully to be in the Bible.

Not so with the spiritually minded. They love God as He really is. Even things about God that are often repulsive to the natural human mind become delightful to the mind set on the things of the Spirit.

Jonathan Edwards wrote in the 1700s how one's view of God changes after conversion. Specifically he reveals how an old hatred for a difficult attribute of God melted into a delight in Him.

> From my childhood up, my mind had been full of objec-
> tions against the doctrine of God's sovereignty in choosing
> whom He would to eternal life. . . . It used to appear like a
> horrible doctrine to me. But I have often, since that first
> conviction, had quite another kind of sense of God's sover-
> eignty than I had then. I have often since had not only a
> conviction, but a delightful conviction. The doctrine has
> very often appeared exceeding pleasant, bright, and sweet.
> Absolute sovereignty is what I love to ascribe to God. But
> my first conviction was not so.[2]

Do you love God for who He is? Do you delight in all He has revealed about Himself? Do you enjoy even the mysterious parts of God's character so much that you can never get enough of knowing Him? Do thoughts of Heaven, and of seeing God there in His holiness and glory, sometimes ravish your heart, mind, and soul? Then your mind is "set on what the Spirit desires."

## YOU ARE *NOT* SPIRITUALLY MINDED
## IF "GOD IS NOT IN ALL [YOUR] THOUGHTS"

Psalm 10 was written by David and is often subtitled, "A Prayer for the Overthrow of the Wicked." Writing under the inspiration of the Holy Spirit, David described a wicked person this way in verse 4: "God is not in all his thoughts" (KJV).

We don't use the word *wicked* very much anymore. To the ears of our culture, describing someone as wicked sounds outdated at best, arrogant at worst. But the Bible uses it to describe all those who have not come in repentance and faith to Jesus Christ. And it says that the distinctive characteristic of the wicked is that this person is not spiritually minded. "God is not in all his thoughts."

Those who aren't spiritually minded think of many things, but they rarely think of God, particularly as He's revealed Himself in Scripture. They never consider God in their plans. They don't consult God for His will. They never wonder if their lives please and honor Him. If somehow their thoughts were projected onto a tiny television screen on their foreheads, you would *rarely* see an earnest thought about God. He may be in their minds occasionally, but God is not in *all* their thoughts.

The godly Puritan thinker, John Owen, observed in "The Grace and Duty of Being Spiritually Minded" that there are degrees of not having God in all one's thoughts.

Some, he says, do not have God in their thoughts because they do not believe God exists. They are the most extreme form of those who do not have God in all their thoughts—atheists. They have their eyes tightly shut to God and the things of God.

However, almost everyone does believe God exists. But of this overwhelming majority, there are many who "claim to know God," but as Titus 1:16 puts it, "by their actions they deny him." Most of them would vehemently affirm that they believe in God, yet they think and live as though God doesn't exist. But they could not have God in all their thoughts and persist lifelong in acting as they do. So despite their words, those in this second group prove by their deeds that "God is not in all [their] thoughts."

Still others *think* they are spiritually minded, but God is in relatively few of their thoughts because "the worries of this life, the deceitfulness of wealth and the desires for other things come in" (Mark 4:19). These folks may know much about the Bible and do many good works both inside and outside the church. They may enjoy the forms of worship because they ease their consciences, and coming to church just makes them "feel better." Because in these ways they have responded to the Word of God and are more familiar with spiritual matters than most people, when they hear about being spiritually minded they assume that they are. But in reality, they think more spontaneously, predominantly, and joyfully about "worries, . . . and wealth, and . . . desires for other things" than the things of God. In truth, "God is not in all [their] thoughts."

The thoughts of nonChristians and Christians are fundamentally different. "Those who live according to the sinful nature have their minds set on what that nature desires," and so "God is not in all [their] thoughts." The spiritually minded "have their minds set on what the Spirit desires," and as a result they think of God spontaneously, abundantly, and with more delight than anything else.

## MORE APPLICATION

*Are you spiritually minded?* Is God a magnet for your mind? Are you finding thoughts about spiritual things simply irrepressible? Do you often become delightfully absorbed in thinking about Jesus Christ, Heaven, the Bible, or other things of God? Take heart! That's the way a Christian thinks.

*God will change the thinking of all who come to Jesus Christ.* If God is not in all your thoughts, He can be. But only the Holy Spirit can put Him there. Will you submit your mind to Him? Will you repent of living according to your sinful nature and of having your mind set on what that nature desires? Will you trust Christ to bring you to God the Father and His transforming power? If so, you will experience the promise God made to all who come to Him through Christ: "I will put my laws in their minds" (Hebrews 8:10).

In 1987, Minnesota Twins' superstar Kirby Puckett lived my childhood fantasy of baseball glory. He led his team to the championship in the last game of the World Series. A few weeks later, I heard an interview with Greg Gagne, the Twins' short-stop. Gagne was asked to describe the scene in the victorious clubhouse after the dramatic victory. He recounted the shouting, the jubilant hugging, the pouring of champagne over each other's heads, etc. But what he remembered most was an eye-snagging glance at a surprisingly silent Puckett only about ten minutes into the celebration. Gagne picked his way through the players and media to the Series star, sitting conspicuously quiet at his locker, and inquired. "If this is all there is to it," Puckett lamented, "life is pretty empty."

Ultimately *every* fantasy is empty except great thoughts of God and the things that are eternal. Fantasy is defined first as "imagination, especially when extravagant and unrestrained." God is so great and glorious that no one can imagine, even in his or her most extravagant and unrestrained thinking, how fantastic the *reality* will be to see Him and live with Him forever in Heaven. But how the spiritually minded delight in trying!

---

NOTES

1. John Owen, *The Works of John Owen*, vol. 7 (London: Johnstone and Hunter, 1850–53; reprint, Edinburgh: The Banner of Truth Trust, 1965), pages 262-497.
2. Iain Murray, *Jonathan Edwards: A New Biography* (Edinburgh: The Banner of Truth Trust, 1987), page 103.

# SEVEN

# THINGS THAT ERODE OUR ASSURANCE

─────── ✝ ───────

*If you have assurance, be careful you do not lose it.*
THOMAS WATSON
*A Body of Divinity*

Let's think again about Christian, the "pilgrim" in John Bunyan's *Pilgrim's Progress*. He is making his way along the Kingshighway to the Celestial City, a pilgrimage that represents the journey through this world by a follower of Christ toward Heaven.

Not long after Christian encounters the Cross of Jesus, where his burden of sin rolls from him, the pilgrim comes upon a hill called Difficulty. He hikes halfway up, then stops at a shaded area to rest. Reclining in the coolness of the arbor, he rereads a scroll given to him at the Cross. In Bunyan's allegory of the Christian life, this scroll represents the promises of God for salvation and the assurance of entrance into Heaven. But while the pilgrim sleeps, the scroll falls from his hand.

Christian awakes suddenly to discover that it is getting dark, and he has far to go before the night. As he hurries, he is accosted by two men running the opposite way. They press Christian to turn back, warning him of danger ahead. Now he is frightened and unsure of what do. He knows he can't return to his home, the City of Destruction, for he realizes God's judgment will fall on that place. Yet there is so much uncertainty before him. Needing comfort and assurance, the pilgrim reaches into his shirt for the scroll. But his assurance is gone! This part of Bunyan's story shows us what many have experienced (discussed in chapter 2), namely, that a true Christian may lose a sense of his or her assurance of salvation.

Notice that I said a true Christian may lose a *sense* of his or her *assurance* of salvation. I did not say a Christian may lose his or her *salvation*. The Bible does not teach that. Once you are born again spiritually into the family of God, you cannot die spiritually. Once God has adopted you into His family, He does not disown or reject you.

But it is possible for a genuine Christian, one who truly has become a child of God, to lose the sense of assurance that he or she is God's own and will one day live with his or her heavenly Father in God's Celestial City.

How can one in whom the Spirit of God permanently resides lose that sense of assurance that God's Spirit *does* live within him or her? How can the genuine Christian, who was once so sure about being on the right path, lose that certainty?

There are at least six ways that it can happen.

## A TRUE CHRISTIAN MAY LOSE A SENSE
## OF ASSURANCE OF SALVATION BECAUSE HE OR SHE
## REFUSES TO DEAL WITH KNOWN SIN

Although I touched on this in chapter 2, it is so important and *so common* that I must address it again.

When we continue to do what God has shown us to be sin against Him, and when we persist in that sin even though our conscience cries out against us, it should come as no surprise that we lose our sense of assurance.

Willful, unrepentant sin grieves the Holy Spirit, the very One who ministers God's assurance to us. The Apostle Paul warns of this in Ephesians 4:30—"Do not grieve the Holy Spirit of God, with whom you were sealed for the day of redemption." Our sin—particularly deliberate or remorseless sin—grieves the Spirit. Whenever that happens, His ministry to us is not to assure us in our sin but to convict us of it.

When we continue in known sin, we're living like an unbeliever. And God will not encourage us in our disobedience. He won't give us a strong sense of assurance that we're His when we intentionally and impenitently live like those who *aren't* His.

It is useless even to ask God for assurance when our greater need is obedience. "If I regard wickedness in my heart," states Psalm 66:18, "the LORD will not hear" (NASB). If our heart clings to sin, the Lord will not hear our prayers for assurance that we have been delivered from it. "Assurance has a narrow throat," said a clever old Englishman, "and may be choked with a small sin." [1]

Obstinate sin corrodes peace and assurance. Repeatedly the Scripture forebodes, "'There is no peace,' says the LORD, 'for the wicked'" (Isaiah 48:22). Although that verse speaks of unbelievers, it contains a principle that is operative for the Christian also. God won't give us the peaceful assurance of Christians while we rebel like the wicked. What He will give us is loving discipline. "The Lord disciplines those he loves," the words of Hebrews 12:6 remind us. Through conviction, rebuke from Scripture or a fellow Christian, "adverse" circumstances, or some other means, the Lord will work to draw us out of sin and back to obedience. But even from this we can derive assurance (cf. Hebrews 12:8).

## A TRUE CHRISTIAN MAY LOSE A SENSE OF ASSURANCE OF SALVATION BECAUSE OF SPIRITUAL LAZINESS

Richard Sibbes, a winsomely Christlike British Puritan of the 1500s and 1600s, observed, "It is the lazy Christian commonly that lacks assurance." [2] Who is the lazy Christian? Lazy Christians are believers sliding on a downgrade to indifference about the spiritual disciplines of the Christian life. When they don't "feel like" reading the Bible, praying, attending public worship, serving in the church, etc., they'll neglect doing so. More and more, other activities take precedence over the things of God in their lives. At first these other things—work, time with others, home chores, school, errands—seem to interfere only occasionally. Gradually they become the norm. Eventually there is always some pressing matter that serves to excuse them from spiritual duties and responsibilities. More often than not, however, the excuse proffered is simply, "I'm too tired."

Lazy Christians never can find time to read a meaty Christian book, but read novels, newspapers, and newsmagazines. They'll watch an hour of television per day, not realizing that totals seven hours per week—ten or more during football season—but still complain of not having an extra hour or more for strengthening the ministry of the church or reaching others. Instead of a life characterized by sacrifice for Christ, the discipleship of the lazy becomes a Christianity of convenience.

So it's no surprise when the spiritually lethargic begin to lose confidence. And they should not be surprised that God gives assurance to the diligent and not to spiritual sloths.

As I write this, Caffy is expecting a baby. She has been feeling our child move for only a short time. For several hours today she was concerned because she didn't feel any activity. Finally the baby moved, and the assurance that there is life within her returned. Spiritual assurance is like that. The less active the Christian, the more he or she may wonder about the presence of spiritual life within. Put another way, the assurance of spiritual life is best noticed in the activity of spiritual life.

Those who *serve Christ* and His Kingdom are the ones who get the most assurance that they *are God's servants*. Those who devote themselves to the *disciplines of Christ* receive the most assurance that they *are disciples of Christ*. Those who *act like children of God* will be given the most assurance that they *are in the family of God*.

If you are lacking assurance, could spiritual laziness be a contributing cause? If so, heed Jonathan Edwards' thoughtful advice: "Assurance is not to be obtained so much by self-examination as by action." [3]

## A TRUE CHRISTIAN MAY LOSE A SENSE OF ASSURANCE OF SALVATION BECAUSE OF SATANIC ATTACKS

In the days of pirate ships, the raiders preferred to attack the ships filled with the greatest riches. Satan, the spiritual pirate, loves to attack those Christians filled with the riches of assurance.

Right after Jesus heard the Father say those assuring words, "This is my Son, whom I love; with him I am well pleased" (Matthew 3:17), Satan attacked Him in the wilderness. Right after the Apostle Paul was given that incredibly assuring experience of being caught up into the third heaven, he confided that "a messenger of Satan" came to buffet him (2 Corinthians 12:7).

Satan hates the people of God. He is sure he will spend eternity in hell, and he hates for Christians to be sure they are going to Heaven. He knows they are most effective when they're sure of their salvation, and ineffective when they're not. The Devil's diabolical strategy, in general, is to convince lost people that they are saved and saved people that they are lost. When Satan tries to get Christians to doubt their salvation, he often attempts to get them to rely on feelings of salvation. Immediately after conversion, many Christians experience a new sense of freedom and spiritual exhilaration. But when it wanes, as it inevitably does, doubts of salvation are common.

Determining the reality of salvation by feelings is a vicious cycle. Although assurance never seems more "real" than when you "feel" it, it never seems more distant than when you don't. If this were the true method of measuring spirituality, it would mean that we can be saved and lost repeatedly—having *eternal* life, then losing it, almost on a moment-by-moment basis.

The Assurance-Hater also tries to get Christians to question their salvation by tempting them to concentrate on their sin instead of on Christ. He succeeds whenever we wonder if all our sin—or a particular sin—is greater than the power of Christ's blood to remove it. It's right to understand what Christians used to call "the sinfulness of sin," as well as realize how it shames us in the sight of God. But we fall into a twisted sense of self-centeredness whenever we focus more on our sin than on Jesus Christ, the Sin-Bearer sent from God.

Another assurance-stealing plot of Satan is to blitz us with his accusations and denials. When Satan attacks your assurance, he usually makes charges like, "If you really were a Christian, you wouldn't do (say, think) that." He knows we are most vulnerable to doubting our salvation when we sin. The antidote is the application of 1 John 1:8-9, which begins with a reminder that every Christian sins, and concludes with the promise of God's forgiveness for every sin of every Christian: "If we claim to be without sin, we deceive ourselves and the truth is not in us. If we confess our sins, he is faithful and just and will forgive us our sins and purify us from all unrighteousness."

As mentioned in chapter 2, one other Satanic scheme to steal assurance from Christians is his attempt to inflate the maturity or blessings of others in comparison with our own. More than one Christian has read the life of some great saint like George Mueller and thought, *If this is what it means to be a Christian, then I am not converted.* Or they might observe the Christlikeness of a contemporary veteran believer, or measure the meagerness of God's apparent blessing upon their lives in contrast with others', and assume that the difference can only be explained by their lack of God's Spirit.

With each of these hellish ploys, victory is experienced by *reinforcing the truth.* After the resurrection of Jesus, but before His disciples had seen him, the Lord appears to two believers walking home from Jerusalem to Emmaus. "But they were kept from recognizing him," reports Luke in 24:16. The gospel writer/physician describes the pair as having "faces downcast" (verse 17). Why? They "had hoped that [Jesus] was the one who was going to redeem Israel" (verse 21). But He had been crucified, "and what is more, it is the third day since all this took place" (verse 21). Their doubts about Jesus and their relationship to Him are just like our struggles with assurance.

How did Jesus restore their assurance? He reinforced the truth in their minds.

> He said to them, "How foolish you are, and how slow of heart to believe all that the prophets have spoken! Did not the Christ have to suffer these things and then enter his glory?" And beginning with Moses and all the Prophets, he

explained to them what was said in all the Scriptures concerning himself. (verses 25-27)

Later, when Jesus had revealed His identity to them, they said to each other, "Were not our hearts burning within us while he talked with us on the road and opened the Scriptures to us?" (verse 32).

When Satan tempted Jesus in Matthew 4:1-11, the Lord responded with the truth—God's Word. When Satan tempts Christians to doubt their relationship to God by relying on feelings, looking at their sin, listening to lies, or comparing themselves with others, believers must reinforce the *truth*. The Devil is a liar and the father of all lies (John 8:44). He is so clever that he can cause any Christian to doubt his or her salvation if the disciple does not remind himself or herself of the truth of God's promises regarding salvation.

## A TRUE CHRISTIAN MAY LOSE A SENSE OF ASSURANCE OF SALVATION BECAUSE OF TRIALS OR HARSH CIRCUMSTANCES

God sometimes allows trials or circumstances so difficult that we feel (to a much lesser degree, of course) like Jesus on the cross when He said, "My God, my God, why have you forsaken me?" (Matthew 27:46). Occasionally things get so bad that some Christians are tempted to believe that God has rejected them. Their conclusion is that their circumstances are a sign of God's displeasure and that possibly He never accepted them in the first place.

Many Christians endure things so painful that they think, *God is against me! How could He allow* this *to happen if He were for me? How could God love me and allow me to hurt so badly and suffer so much? I wouldn't do this to* my *child. How can I be a child of God when He allows this to happen to me?* And so they think they have reason to believe they are not in God's family.

Some will begin to wonder about whether they are children of God when He allows them to be greatly disappointed.

Through a broken relationship perhaps, or a desired relationship that never happens, or a death, or a miscarriage, or childlessness. Disappointment may come when someone else gets the job or the transfer, or when *you* get the transfer. You may be disillusioned with your marriage, or with your children. And before long you are tempted to think, *If I really am a Christian, how could God let this happen to me?*

Maybe you prayed for one thing and got just the opposite. Possibly all your expectations for the future were dashed. Perhaps you've lost your job or your money, or there's been an accident, or your children are sick, or your friends have turned on you. Maybe you've been verbally or physically or sexually abused. Does any of this mean God is against you? Even if a combination of these things happen to you, did they occur because you're not a Christian and He is out to get you?

For the Christian, God is in everything somehow. He promises to cause "all things to work together for good to those who love [Him], to those who are called according to His purpose" (Romans 8:28, NASB), even though we cannot perceive the "good" in many things that happen on this side of Heaven. Regardless of how horrible the event, there are no "accidents" when there is a *sovereign* God. No matter how evidently Satan is involved, he never operates beyond God's leash. After all, as Stephen Charnock emphasized, "Satan is God's ape." [4] As the story of Job teaches us, the Devil can do nothing without God's approval or apart from His purposes.

But from our perspective, the reality of God's control is not measured by the visibility of His hand. We must remember the declaration of Psalm 119:91, "For all things serve you." Just as a porpoise in the Pacific is surrounded with water, so the Scripture says of our omnipresent, omnipotent God, "In him we live and move and have our being" (Acts 17:28). How does this relate to assurance of salvation? It means that *true Christians* go through some of the worst trials and harshest circumstances in this world. Also, it's wrong to doubt God's acceptance of you just because you feel He's rejected your prayers or allowed your heart and life to be broken. Even Jesus experienced the loss of a loved one. He was rejected by those to whom He was *perfect*. God allowed Him to be brokenhearted. He knew what it was like to hurt, even to the point of weeping with grief. Jesus, too, saw His friends abandon him.

Listen to Hebrews 12:5-6—

> "My son, do not make light of the Lord's discipline, and do not lose heart when he rebukes you, because the Lord disciplines those he loves, and he punishes everyone he accepts as a son."

The truth is, the "discipline" of God is a biblical sign that God *does* love you and receive you. As verse 5 states, don't "lose heart" at these things. Don't let them steal your assurance. Instead, let them *give* you assurance.

## A TRUE CHRISTIAN MAY LOSE A SENSE OF ASSURANCE OF SALVATION BECAUSE OF ILLNESS OR TEMPERAMENT

Some Christians, who never doubted their salvation before, lose their assurance when they become very sick or are near death. And there are some who are more prone than others to doubting their relationship with God just because of their mental and emotional makeup.

You'd be amazed at how many great and godly Christians, people who normally stood as solid as a statue in a thunderstorm regarding the assurance of their salvation, had serious doubts about it when they came to die. Of course, there are some people who reveal their longstanding hypocrisy in moments like this. But it is possible for genuine Christians to panic when they are very sick and wonder if their souls are safe. It can be a fearful thing to have the reality of death and judgment suddenly come upon you. And a sick or painful body may affect the way you think. Even though God frequently gives unusual calm and peace to those who are seriously ill, some genuine Christians die in doubt and anxiety.

When sick people lose a sense of the assurance, often it's because they look backward to their salvation experience and wonder if they understood enough, if they were sincere enough, etc. They wonder if they have sufficiently responded to Christ.

But as a sick person or a healthy one, if you ever doubt that you came to Christ before, come to Him *now*. Instead of worrying about what happened in the past, repent and believe now. If Jesus accepted the faith of the thief on the cross, He will accept your faith in your illness and weakness.

Occasionally, there are those who can never accept assurance because of mental illness. Their doubts may be related to organic psychological problems, imbalance in brain chemistry, or other such causes. In such cases, medical attention is needed in addition to sound counseling.

A more common problem, however, is that of experiencing assurance due to temperament. Probably the greatest pastor among the English Puritans was Richard Baxter. He is the model for pastors when it comes to the care of souls, and his books on pastoral ministry still sell by the thousands even after 350 years. Baxter said he had long observed that a melancholic temperament was the "commonest cause" of deep and long periods of lack of assurance among godly people.[5] Some people are more cheerful by temperament and others are more gloomy. Some are naturally more optimistic in their outlook and others succumb more easily to depression. Some do not evaluate themselves and consider their ways enough, while others are by nature overly introspective. And it is inevitable that those who tend toward the latter categories will be more prone to doubts about their salvation. Those who are temperamentally more cheerful can hardly imagine people wrestling for long periods about their salvation, and those who are more melancholy by nature can hardly fathom what it would be like to have a strong assurance of salvation.

One Christian of melancholic termperament was William Cowper, who lived in England from 1731 to 1800. A one-paragraph biography in *Who Was Who in Church History* says he was "naturally inclined to morbid brooding and worry. . . . [He] was prey to very deep religious doubts . . . and often fell into deep depression. The last decade or more of his life was a period of deep gloom and a settled notion that God had cast him off." [6]

Although he battled a lack of assurance all his life, Cowper dealt with his doubts in the right way. He had his highs and lows, but he fought hard to gain assurance, and he reinforced his doubts with the truth. Because of this, he had times of walking in the sunshine of assurance, and God has used his struggles to bless millions of Christians ever since. For it was William Cowper who wrote these immortal lines of assurance and faith:

> God moves in a mysterious way
> His wonders to perform;
> He plants His footsteps in the sea
> And rides upon the storm.

> You fearful saints, fresh courage take:
> The clouds you so much dread
> Are big with mercy, and shall break
> In blessings on your head.

> Judge not the Lord by feeble sense,
> But trust Him for His grace;
> Behind a frowning providence
> He hides a smiling face.

> Blind unbelief is sure to err
> And scan His work in vain;
> God is His own interpreter,
> And He will make it plain.

William Cowper also penned these confident words:

> There is a fountain filled with blood
> Drawn from Immanuel's veins;
> And sinners, plunged beneath that flood,
> Lose all their guilty stains.

If you are prone to overexamining every thought and word and deed and motive, you are focusing too much on yourself. Again, this is an inverted self-centeredness. It is focusing on yourself when you should be focusing on God and the work of Christ. It's as though you've taken a giant telescope, which should be pointing heavenward, and turned it upon yourself. If you overdo that, you'll always find things that depress you, because you'll always find sin and things that should not be a part of a Christian's life. Instead, fix your lens upon God and focus on Him and what Jesus Christ has done.

## A TRUE CHRISTIAN MAY LOSE A SENSE OF ASSURANCE OF SALVATION BECAUSE GOD SEEMS TO WITHDRAW A SENSE OF HIS PRESENCE AND BLESSING

Every Christian goes through times of spiritual dryness. Our evangelical forefathers used to refer to these times as God's desertions, times where it appears and feels as though God has deserted you.

What do you do when you know that Jesus said He would never leave nor forsake His own, and yet you feel as though He's forsaken you? Well, some start thinking they are not Jesus' own. What are we to think when God doesn't seem to hear our prayers? What are we to think when we read the Bible or come to worship and don't sense God at all? What are we to think when the blessing of God, which was so evident in times past, seems to be removed from us, from our ministry, from our family?

It's so easy to be sure of your salvation when God is dramatically answering prayer, when in worship it seems as though you could reach out and feel the folds of His robe, when He is obviously blessing your life and ministry. But it isn't easy to be as sure when all these things are gone.

Psalm 102:1-7 describes how a true believer feels when God seems to have turned His back:

Hear my prayer, O LORD;
    let my cry for help come to you.
Do not hide your face from me

when I am in distress.
Turn your ear to me;
    when I call, answer me quickly.
For my days vanish like smoke;
    my bones burn like glowing embers.
My heart is blighted and withered like grass;
    I forget to eat my food.
Because of the loud groaning
    I am reduced to skin and bones.
I am like a desert owl,
    like an owl among the ruins.
I lie awake; I have become
    like a bird alone on a roof.

True believers can still feel the same way today. And when they do, they aren't as sure that God has saved them.

Why does God do that? First, we must remember that He doesn't really leave us. My street is lined with old maples, and leaf-heavy branches stretch to each other across the blacktop. When I take walks on sunny days, I'll stroll through bright spots and shady ones. The sun is just as near in both. In our Christian walk we often feel the light and warmth of God's nearness, yet there are times when we don't. But even when we can't sense the warmth of His presence, and spiritual things seem darker, God is just as near as ever.

However, sometimes He does withdraw an *awareness* of His presence, or we may sin away a *sense* of His blessing, but once He enters us at salvation He never leaves (Hebrews 13:5). One reason, though, why He does seem to withdraw is so we might learn to "live by faith, not by sight" (2 Corinthians 5:7), and to rest our assurance on nothing but Christ.

It is so natural for us to want to attach our assurance to emotions, memorable experiences, spiritual gifts, the evidence of His blessing, or the pronouncements of parents, pastors, or an evangelist. God wants us to learn to trust in His character and in the work of Jesus Christ alone.

He also wants us to learn to walk by faith in the darkness and not by feelings in the light. It's easy to stay faithful when prayers are dramatically answered, when worship is intoxicating, and when everything in the Christian life is exciting. But there are times when He wants us to pray even when He doesn't appear to answer, to obey when He doesn't seem to bless obedience.

Stiffen your wavering assurance with the truth. "Why are you downcast, O my soul?" asked the writer of Psalm 42:5,

> Why so disturbed within me?
> Put your hope in God,
> > for I will yet praise him,
> > my Savior and my God.

## MORE APPLICATION

*Those who consistently repent of all known sin are the ones most likely to receive the assurance that they are saved from sin.* Because sin has affected every part of us, nothing we do, say, or think is totally pure from sin. But it's one thing to speak of always having sin in our lives this way, and another to be convicted by the Holy Spirit of a specific sin and persistently refusing to deal with it. If you are lacking assurance, is there something God has plainly told you to do and you have refused? "Do not put out the Spirit's fire" admonishes 1 Thessalonians 5:19. When the Holy Spirit kindles a fire of conviction in your heart and you throw water on it, no wonder there is no assurance. But the Lord wants us to have assurance. We don't *earn* it by obeying Him, but He usually crowns obedience with assurance.

*Those who shake off spiritual laziness through the disciplines and duties of a disciple of Jesus are the ones most likely to receive the assurance that they are saved by Jesus.* Jesus told the Jews who believed in Him, "If you hold to my teaching, you are really my disciples" (John 8:31). Those who are actively obedient to the teaching of Jesus are the ones most likely to receive the assurance of really being disciples of Jesus. Of course, doing what a Christian does will not make anyone a Christian, but assurance will not come to anyone who does *not* do what the Bible says a Christian does.

*Those who recognize and fight against Satanic attacks are the ones most likely to receive the assurance that they are saved from Satan's power.* Regarding the Devil's plans, we may confidently assert with Paul, "We are not unaware of his schemes" (2 Corinthians 2:11). We know he intends to pirate our assurance. Fight him with the flintlike truth. Temper your assurance with fiery texts like Romans 8:33-34—"Who will bring any charge against those whom God has chosen? It is God who justifies. Who is he that condemns? Christ Jesus, who died—more than that, who was raised to life—is at the right hand of God and is also interceding for us."

*Those who continue to trust God and to persevere in faith during trials and harsh circumstances are the ones most likely to receive the assurance that they are saved from eternal punishment.* As difficult as it may be for you to remain firm in faith right now, don't give up. Perseverance is the path to assurance. Like faith, assurance grows only when it is tested. Don't let any trial or circumstance, no matter how hard or how long, cause you to doubt the love of Jesus for you.

*Those who continue to rest in the character of God, the work of Jesus Christ, and the promises of Scripture despite sickness or temperament are the ones most likely to receive the assurance that they are saved from eternal agony.* If you struggle with assurance because of your physical or emotional or temperamental condition, you must learn to rest in the truth or you will always grope for assurance. Some grow weary of the battle and decide that either God has rejected them or the possibility of assurance is a cruel hoax. Accept neither option. Make sure you reinforce the truth of God's character, Christ's work, and Scripture's promises through the means of preaching, fellowship, and reading time-tested Christian literature.

*Those who continue to obey God and walk by faith when God seems to desert them are the ones most likely to receive the assurance that they are saved from eternal separation from God.* As you continue living for the glory of God, despite a lack of assurance, you will soon see your assurance return. As you honor and glorify God by obeying Him even without a sense of assurance, you show that you put God's interests before your own, even your own desire for assurance. God loves to give assurance to people like that. Who else but a child of God would be willing to persevere in obedience without the feeling of God's blessing on it or the sense of being rewarded for it?

Remember Christian from *Pilgrim's Progress*? When we left him, he had just discovered that the scroll that gave him the assurance of entrance into the Celestial City was missing. As he considered where it might be, he determined that it must be in the place where he fell asleep. He recovered his assurance only by returning to the place where he lost it.

Have you lost your assurance? Where did you lose it? Return to that place, for there will you find assurance again.

NOTES
1. Thomas Fuller, as quoted in John Blanchard, comp., *Gathered Gold* (Welwyn, England: Evangelical Press, 1984), page 7.
2. Richard Sibbes, as quoted in Richard Baxter, *The Practical Works of Richard Baxter*, vol. 3, *The Saints' Everlasting Rest* (reprint, Ligonier, PA: Soli Deo Gloria, 1990), page 179.
3. Jonathan Edwards, as quoted in John Gerstner, *The Rational Biblical Theology of Jonathan Edwards*, vol. 3 (Powhatan, VA: Berea Publications; Orlando, FL: Ligonier Ministries, 1993), page 343.
4. Blanchard, page 273.
5. Richard Baxter, *The Practical Works of Richard Baxter*, vol. 1, *A Christian Directory* (reprint, Ligonier, PA: Soli Deo Gloria, 1990), page 503.
6. Elgin S. Moyer, ed., *Who Was Who in Church History* (New Canaan, CT: Keaths Publishing, 1974), page 104.

# EIGHT

# COMMON PROBLEMS
# WITH UNCERTAINTY

✝

*The facts are that the more . . . unwavering the assurance*
*of salvation is, the humbler, the more stable and the more*
*circumspect will be the life, walk and conduct.*
JOHN MURRAY
*The Collected Writings of John Murray*

Several years ago, I visited a family to gain insight into the spiritual condition of the seven-year-old daughter, who'd made a profession of faith in Christ. As is my practice, I posed several questions and was proceeding carefully.

To determine how well she comprehended separation from God and the importance of the gospel, I asked, "Is *everyone* a Christian?"

To discern what she knew of sin, I asked softly, "What is sin?" and "Do you sin?"

To see how well she understood the gospel, I drew her out gently with, "Suppose one of your friends said to you, 'I want to be a Christian too.' What would you tell her?"

With sensitive inquiries, I sought to know if she not only had a sense of loving Jesus (even three-year-olds in Sunday school would eagerly say they do), but also of *needing* Jesus.

Then I turned to the parents and said, "You see her every day and obviously know her much better than I. Have you perceived any changes since her profession of faith? In ways that only a parent might notice, have you observed more sensitivity to sin, or more of a hunger for spiritual things, or an increased desire to please God?"

I could see by the growing impatience on the mother's face that she did not understand the need for this discussion. She expected me to baptize her daughter the next Sunday, simply upon the child's willingness to say she'd "asked Jesus into her heart" (a phrase I'll comment on later).

Her attitude changed, though, when I said, "One reason I am so cautious with children is that I don't want those who are genuinely born again to struggle later with doubts about the reality of their childhood conversion. If your daughter has not really understood and responded to the gospel, we need to know that. But if God has saved her, she will benefit both now and later if we can help her articulate her experience with Him."

That's when the mother revealed that she, too, had made a profession of faith as a child. But ever since her teenage years, she had been savaged with doubts about whether she had truly been saved at that early age. Embarrassed still to be unsure about her salvation after all these years, she had never discussed her private turmoil with anyone. However, she was very willing to help her daughter avoid following in her agony.

This story is typical of several common problems regarding assurance of salvation that are addressed in this chapter.

## THOSE CONVERTED AS CHILDREN MAY EXPERIENCE SPECIAL DIFFICULTIES WITH ASSURANCE

During an after-church, fellowship/theological-discussion meeting in our home, a woman admitted, "I just can't understand how anyone who is born again could ever have doubts about it."

At first her remark concerned me, but then I understood how she could say this. Presently in her forties, she wasn't brought to faith in Christ until her late thirties. She had been raised in a ritualistic religious environment, but by the time she finished college she was an atheist. She persisted in denying God's existence for fifteen years, all the while reading philosophy and psychology in search of answers. When God opened her eyes to the truth of the gospel and brought her to Himself, her mind and life were suddenly turned rightside-up. She was transferred so quickly and clearly from darkness into light, and was so dramatically changed, that she has never had one doubt about her salvation.

Hearing her testimony made me realize that those whose conversion experience is like hers may, like her, have fewer struggles with assurance. On the other hand, it also made me think of the reverse side of the coin.

## Those Who Remember Little Else Besides Following Christ Sometimes Have Doubts That Those with Adult or Dramatic Conversions Do Not

The Lord convicted me of my sin and need for Christ, drew me to Himself, and saved me when I was nine years old. I was raised in a Christian home and a Bible-preaching church, and I have never really known what it was like to be secular in viewpoint and ungodly in lifestyle. I can't remember too much of what it was like *not* to be a Christian, and everything in my life before then was influenced by Christianity and the Bible. The change in my life wasn't as unmistakable and dramatic as many who repented and believed as adults. And although I am very grateful for the advantages of knowing Christ from my childhood, an early conversion can produce questions later. There is the propensity to wonder, "All my life I've only known one way of living. Is my Christianity merely 'cultural' or am I really converted?"

Why do those who remember little else besides following Christ sometimes have doubts that those with adult or dramatic conversions do not? One reason is because those saved as children aren't able to contrast their lives before and after salvation as clearly as can those converted as adults.

When you can vividly remember what it was like to be in sin and apart from Christ for years, and you can point to countless ways your life has changed since then, it may be easier for you to be assured of your salvation than for someone who can only remember one way of living and thinking. Those of us who have known the way of God and the Scriptures from our youth may compare our experience with the testimony of those converted later in life and wonder, because our experience is so different, whether we've had the same salvation.

As I've already emphasized, the reality of salvation is not

demonstrated so much by the experience at the beginning as by the fruit since then. What counts is not so much what you said or did then but what you believe and practice now. It is not the *backward* look that is important in gaining assurance of salvation, but the look at what you believe and are doing *now*.

## Concrete Childhood Thinking Differs
## from More Abstract Adult Thinking

We think more concretely as children and learn to reason about more abstract concepts only as we mature. For instance, a nine-year-old boy can understand what it means to obey what Jesus says in the Bible, and yet he may not be able to explain much more than that about the lordship of Christ. He may understand that Jesus died in his place and brought about the forgiveness of his sins, but grasp little of what the words *propitiation* or *atonement* mean when he reads them in Scripture. God may give a child the ability to repent and believe in Jesus before he can analyze the terms with the depth of an adult's understanding of them.

This is why I don't like to talk to children about "asking Jesus into your heart." Not only is the phrase never used in the Bible, but I have known children to be afraid of surgery because they didn't want to lose a tiny, tangible Jesus they imagined living inside their physical heart. We shouldn't be afraid to use biblical phrases such as "repent and believe the good news" (Mark 1:15). Sure, children require explanation and illustration to understand them, but so do adults! And if we want to use other descriptions of salvation, let's talk to them about giving their life to Jesus, living for Jesus, doing all that Jesus says, obeying what Jesus says in the Bible, etc.

Frequently, however, children may be born again at an age where their thinking is still predominantly concrete, and five or ten years later develop problems with assurance, just like the mom at the beginning of this chapter. Sometime during their teenage years, when their abstract reasoning is more fully developed, they look back across the years to a time where they thought more simply and wonder if they really understood enough to become a Christian. As a result, they are tormented with doubts about whether they were saved at that age.

Again, the most important thing to do is not to center your attention on how much you knew back then, or how sincere you were at that moment, or on unraveling what your motives were years ago, etc. Endeavoring to confirm your conversion by trying to mentally recreate an experience from years ago is no more necessary than attempting to recall your birth in order to prove that you're alive. The most important thing is to ask, "Do I have the signs of Christian life *now*? Do I love Jesus *today*? Do I trust in Christ as my only hope of salvation, or in my own efforts, or in Christ plus my works?" Knowing the moment of your conversion is inconsequential when compared to knowing simply that you *are* converted.

### An Awareness of the Lordship of Christ Must Expand to Cover All the Ever-Expanding Circle of Life that Comes with Maturity

Here's another reason some of those converted as children may experience difficulty with assurance as they mature: Their awareness of the lordship of Christ doesn't increase with their ever-growing responsibilities and privileges.

Let a small circle represent the entire life of a nine-year-old girl who is born again. She understands that everything in her life belongs to Jesus and that she is to obey Jesus in all those things. But now draw a larger circle around the small circle. This represents the life of that girl at age eighteen. Her life has grown and now includes areas she could not have imagined when she was nine. There are relationships with people of the opposite sex. There is a job, stewardship of a paycheck, decisions about college and career, and much more.

It may be that God withdraws a sense of assurance of salvation from that Christian teenager because some of these areas have never been consciously placed under the lordship of Christ. While spending money she may have never thought, *You know, really this is God's money. I wonder if He is pleased with how I'm using it?* She may have yet to think, *As a Christian, I should have Christ in the center of my relationships with the opposite sex.* Until she begins thinking like a Christian in these areas, she may act in them much like her nonChristian friends. During this time she struggles with a sense of assurance that she is born again. If you were to ask her if she should obey Christ in every area of life, she would immediately answer yes. But in her process of maturing, she has not yet become consciously aware that parts of her life have developed without any consideration of what Jesus would have her do about them.

At this point, the doubts about the reality of her childhood conversion, combined with conviction from the Holy Spirit about her present spiritual condition, often results in a spiritual crisis. Some mistakenly call this "making Christ Lord of your life." It is more accurate, however, to say that she is *returning* to the lordship of Christ over all of life, which is what she gave herself to, however simply, at salvation. She is again deliberately submitting everything in her life to His will, especially those areas where she had not consciously recognized Him before.

Remember that we are describing the experience of someone who was *genuinely* converted as a child. I believe that many, if not most, of those who have a life-changing experience of "making Christ Lord" are actually converted in *that* experience, not in the childhood event. But it's true that many Christians have such an experience, however misnamed, and this can help them understand it.

Such an occurrence can happen to a Christian not only in the teen years, but at eleven or thirty. In fact, in smaller ways it happens throughout the Christian life, as even mature believers repent after they realize they have been doing something without reference to the will of God.

In one sense, this experience is characteristic of daily Christianity, with a believer more fully understanding the application of the lordship of Christ to every detail in life. A woman who's been a Christian for sixty years may suddenly realize that an expression she's used all her life does not honor God. To confess that to God and to begin eliminating it from her vocabulary differs only in degree from the crisis experience of the teenager.

## STAY-AT-HOME MOTHERS OF YOUNG CHILDREN MAY EXPERIENCE SPECIAL DIFFICULTIES WITH ASSURANCE

Stay-at-home moms, in my experience, is another group that seems to have a disproportionately high number of Christians struggling with assurance.

I can only speculate on some of the reasons for this. A woman who feels as though changing diapers, cleaning messes, and chasing children to feed, bathe, and bed them down isn't as important as a career outside the home is subjecting herself to doubts of all kinds, including spiritual ones.

This is another situation where the solution involves reinforcing the mind with the truth. The plain truth is that an outside career is *not* more significant than being a Christian mom at home. Moms will not see daily or monthly bottom-line results, as those in the marketplace often do, and that also can contribute to a lack of assurance.

I could write more about how the stay-at-home mom needs to take the long-range view of her impact, but that has been better said elsewhere. As this problem relates specifically to assurance, however, my reminder is: Don't let your search for significance as a mom slide into the thinking that God's acceptance of you is based on the importance of your daily activities. He saves people because of His grace, not their goodness. And He has written to us so that *all* "who believe in the name of the Son of God," including stay-at-home moms, "may know that [they] have eternal life" (1 John 5:13).

Other factors behind stay-at-home moms' doubts are more obvious. For one thing, they are *so busy*. Rest is at a premium. Fuse the frequent fatigue with a catch-as-catch-can devotional life and you have someone with the spiritual doubts of the "Elijah Syndrome" (see 1 Kings 19:3-5). In addition to stay-at-home moms, it's not startling for *anyone* with chronic busyness and weariness sometimes to doubt whether he or she has the abundant life Jesus promised to believers (John 10:10).

To make matters worse, the necessities of parenting can often interfere with your regular spiritual input of preaching, teaching, and fellowship. Absence from church due to a child's sickness, rotating church nursery duty, and other responsibilities can accumulate in bunches. This will make your soul thin and dry. Anyone who stays in this condition long—or gets into it often—can easily become discouraged spiritually.

Since it's not likely that things will change drastically until the children are older, it's imperative that you take the initiative to reestablish contact with the resources that encourage assurance. Get as much spiritual refreshment as possible in the home. Make a commitment to read one chapter, or at least one paragraph, from the Bible each day. I heard of one mom who left open Bibles in every room where she spent a lot of time so it would be easy to pick up Scriptures and read. Even if some days you have to read it while stirring the soup or aloud to your child so as to have time, refuse to excuse yourself from the Word of God.

Another suggestion is to bring Bible teaching into your home through Christian radio or tapes. Your pastor or others in your church will have a helpful supply of tapes you can borrow, including taped readings of the entire Bible. If possible, attend a women's Bible study that offers child care.

Foster fellowship by inviting another Christian woman or two into your home for coffee or lunch. Make it a weekly thing and rotate the site if necessary. For several summers, a woman in our church organized a "Lunch with a Bunch" each week. At the beginning of the season a list of eight to ten locations, mostly parks, was drawn up in advance. This list was printed, photocopied, and distributed. Each week, all the stay-at-home moms in the church gathered their children and a picnic lunch and met at the designated location. With no cost and little effort, the children had a great playtime and the moms enjoyed fine fellowship.

Being a Christian mother can be draining—physically, emotionally, and spiritually. But that doesn't mean your assurance has to be drained.

## TRUE ASSURANCE WON'T LEAD
## TO SPIRITUAL CARELESSNESS

Those who oppose the teaching of assurance usually argue that it is a dangerous doctrine that will lead to spiritual carelessness. "Let a person become convinced that he is going to Heaven," they will say, "and he won't be as committed. He'll become spiritually slovenly, taking it easy and becoming unconcerned about good works as he coasts into Heaven."

"I know plenty of people," they may say, "who are sure they are going to Heaven, and yet they live like the Devil!" Therefore, they are convinced that to teach people that they can be sure of salvation deceives them and makes them spiritually callous and lazy.

That may be true of the unconverted who have false assurance, but as C. H. Spurgeon shows in this rhetorical dialogue, that's not how the children of God are affected by the certainty of salvation:

> "But," says yet another friend, "if I believed that I was really saved, I should say, 'Now I may live as I like.'" Ah, my friend! there is nothing I should like better than to live as I like, and do you know how I would live if I could live as I liked? I would never sin again. . . . But if you, as an unconverted man, live as you like, I should not like to read the record of your life. But we are not talking about men in general, but about renewed men, those who have been changed by grace, and who have become children of God, who like to live after a very different fashion.[1]

Still, opponents of assurance apparently think it's better to be in doubt about your standing with God, to have your salvation in jeopardy every moment, always living on the edge of God's mercy, never knowing when you might fall away from Him and back into condemnation. They think a lack of assurance about whether you'll finally make it to Heaven or will eventually slip and sink into hell is the best motivator for faithfulness and good works.

But these objections to teaching assurance reveal a view of salvation that is too works-oriented. The Bible does declare that those who know God and will be admitted into Heaven will serve Him and do good works (Matthew 5:16, Ephesians 2:10, Hebrews 12:14, James 2:14-18). But salvation—being made right with God and ready for Heaven—is a result of God's grace (Ephesians 2:8-9). And if salvation is clearly seen as emanating from God's grace, how can assurance of it lead to pride, presumption, spiritual carelessness, etc.? Now if man is the controlling factor in salvation, then salvation is unsure. But if salvation is God's work, becoming sure of what He has done for you will not cut the nerve of your spiritual faithfulness.

The truth is, having assurance of salvation *encourages* and *strengthens* faithfulness. You are so grateful to God that you want to serve Him and live for Him.

If anyone ever had assurance of salvation, it was Paul. But this didn't make him spiritually careless. It made him all the more faithful. And he was never more faithful than when he wrote from prison, "I know whom I have believed, and am convinced that he is able to guard what I have entrusted to him for that day" (2 Timothy 1:12).

Suppose you owed a great debt, perhaps in back taxes after an IRS audit or to the hospital for a catastrophic medical emergency. Then you heard that a certain man was thinking about paying the bill and releasing you from the debt. Wouldn't your commitment to that person be affected by whether he actually pays that bill for you? If you had merely heard that he was *thinking* of paying it, but you weren't sure he had, wouldn't your attitude toward him be different than if you had assurance that he *had* paid the debt? On the one hand, you might go out of your way to do things for him in hopes that he would pay your bill for you, but your motivation would be selfish and your actions done out of fear that he might not pay your bill. But any decent person, upon gaining assurance that the man had paid the bill, would be committed to doing all he could for that man for the rest of his life, simply out of gratitude and love.

That's what Jesus did. He paid an unpayable debt for His people. And those who have the assurance that He died for them and paid their debt to God will not become spiritually careless, but more faithful than ever.

"There is a keener stimulus than the fear of falling," said James W. Alexander, "it is the mingled agency of faith, and hope, and gratitude, and love. He who is surest of the crown, will not be the first to trample on it. He who is certain of meeting Christ, will not be most ready to insult and grieve Him." [2]

## THOSE WORRIED ABOUT THE UNFORGIVABLE SIN HAVE NOT COMMITTED IT

Many Christians wring their hands with uncertainty about whether they have committed the "unforgivable sin." The two passages that refer to this sin are Matthew 12:22-32 and Mark 3:22-30. A demon-possessed man was brought to Jesus, and He cast the demon out of the man. The people who saw it were amazed and began to wonder aloud if Jesus could be the Messiah. "But when the Pharisees heard this," Matthew 12:24 reports, "they said, 'It is only by Beelzebub, the prince of demons, that this fellow drives out demons.'"

Part of Jesus' response to them is recorded in verses 31-32: "I tell you, every sin and blasphemy will be forgiven men, but the blasphemy against the Spirit will not be forgiven. Anyone who speaks a word against the Son of Man will be forgiven, but anyone who speaks against the Holy Spirit will not be forgiven, either in this age or in the age to come."

### What the Unforgivable Sin Is *Not*

Any sin named elsewhere in the Bible is not the unforgivable sin. This sin is unique. For instance, the sin referred to in other texts as idolatry is not the unpardonable sin. It is not called idolatry in one place and the unforgivable sin in Matthew 12:31-32. Idolatry is idolatry, lust is lust, lying is lying, and the unforgivable sin is the unforgivable sin. Any other sin is forgivable, even sins like murder and adultery, both of which were committed by King David and forgiven by God. (Incidentally, let me add that the sin of self-murder, that is, suicide, is not the unforgivable sin, as some have feared. It is possible for a Christian to kill himself or herself, but it is not wise to commit murder as your last act prior to standing before God.)

Nor does any sin become the unforgivable sin after it is committed a certain number of times, as though lying 999 times is forgivable but the 1,000th lie is not. The Bible never gives us numerical limits of forgiveness.

Not even denying Christ or blaspheming Him is beyond the hope of forgiveness. Paul mentions in 1 Timothy 1:13-14 that he was forgiven of blasphemy. In a broad sense, any thought or word against God and His Word is blasphemy. If ever, even for a moment, you doubted the love or power of God, you have blasphemed Him. So in that sense, *every* Christian has been forgiven of blasphemy, both before *and* after salvation.

Although some identify it as such, the unforgivable sin is not persistent unbelief. Certainly those who commit the unforgivable sin do have persistent unbelief, but the two sins are distinguishable. Many in Jesus' day persisted in their rejection of Him, but they were not charged with the unforgivable sin as were those in Matthew 12:31-32.

Neither is speaking flippantly about the Holy Spirit a sin that cannot be forgiven. A friend in ministry told me of an experience of his while a teenager en route to summer church camp. He repeated a joke that included a reference to the Spirit. The driver immediately wrenched the bus off the road, came back, and pointed a finger in the face of the youth. "Don't *ever* make a joke about the Holy Spirit," he solemnly intoned. "You *may* have just committed the unforgivable sin." The terror of that possibility so haunted the Christian young man that thirty years later he remembers wondering if he had inadvertently forfeited his salvation. As I will show, the character of his concern reveals that he did not commit the unforgivable sin.

Although the young man did wrong, what Christian hasn't experienced this irreverent spirit by laughing at something said, perhaps even from a pulpit, that referred at least remotely to the

Holy Spirit? Moreover, what Christian hasn't thought of something else while singing a hymn that included a reference to the Person or work of the Spirit? That is also a flippant, vain, and sinful use of the Holy Spirit's name by people who have had *all* their sins forgiven, so this can't be unforgivable.

To go further, not every known, willful sin against the Spirit is unpardonable. First John 1:8 says of Christians, "If we claim to be without sin, we deceive ourselves and the truth is not in us." And much of the time when we do sin, we do so after the Holy Spirit has warned us that the action we are considering is sinful. Christians are told they can grieve and quench the Holy Spirit (Ephesians 4:30, 1 Thessalonians 5:19), and this must include known, willful sin against Him. Yet God forgives His children of these intentional sins against the Spirit.

Jesus said categorically that "every sin and blasphemy," even if "against the Son of Man," will be forgiven. From the rest of Scripture we know this doesn't mean that all sins will be forgiven automatically and universally. The responsibility of sinners seeking forgiveness is to repent and believe in Christ (Mark 1:15; cf. Colossians 2:13, 1 John 1:7-9). But all who genuinely seek forgiveness will be forgiven of all sins.

**What the Unforgivable Sin Is**
Jesus said the unforgivable sin is "blasphemy against" (Matthew 12:31) or when one "speaks against" the Holy Spirit (verse 32). He indicted the Pharisees present in verses 22-29 with this "because they were saying, 'He has an evil spirit'" (Mark 3:30).

There are two major views about the meaning of the unforgivable sin. One says the sin of blasphemy against the Holy Spirit is calling Christ demonic and His miracles Satanic. It is the specific sin of saying that Jesus was demonized and that what He did was not of God, but the work of the Devil. Those who hold this view rely heavily on the statement of Mark 3:30 that the Pharisees were guilty of an eternal sin "because they were saying, 'He has an evil spirit.'" This narrows the possibility of committing this sin dramatically. It requires language virtually as explicit as the words spoken by the Pharisees.

The other leading interpretation of the unpardonable sin holds that the accusations of the Pharisees represent something broader. Those with this view say it is a verbal, intentional, persistent, and unremorseful rejection of Christ, *despite knowing* the truth about Him *clearly* through the enlightenment of the Holy Spirit. Probably some *open* enmity toward Christ and His work are involved also. This definition makes the unforgivable sin more than the plain and perpetual unbelief characteristic of most unconverted people.

What all this means is, if you are anxious about the unforgivable sin, then you have *not* committed it. Genuine concern about it can be the work of the Holy Spirit, and it is impossible for Spirit-indwelled people (Christians) to commit the unforgivable sin. No one who has the Holy Spirit can ever blaspheme the Holy Spirit. Furthermore, Christians already have all their sins forgiven, so it is impossible for them to commit an unforgivable one.

The Apostle John reminds us that "the blood of Jesus, his [God's] Son, purifies us from all sin" (1 John 1:7). Paul says of God in Colossians 2:13, "He forgave us all our sins." The Bible teaches that Christ's death paid for all the sins of every believer, not all sins except one. When God forgives *all* our sins, He doesn't forgive just our past sins, but all future sins as well. If all future sins are forgiven, there can't be one unforgivable sin in the future of any born-again person.

You may say, "But sometimes I have blasphemous thoughts! Now and then some of the most wicked and shameful things you could ever imagine pop into my head." Occasionally you may even utter some of these things. Yes, but are you glad you have these thoughts or say these words? Do you enjoy them? If you hate them and are repentant, and wish that you would never think or say them, then you haven't committed the unforgivable sin.

You cannot possibly have committed the unforgivable sin if you are concerned that you have committed it. Those who sin the unpardonable sin are unrepentant. They are so hardened that they repeat the sin habitually. Never do they feel even a twinge of remorse. But Christians are terrified to think of such a sin. They would rather die than embrace one pardonless sin. If that's your attitude, you are not guilty.

## MORE APPLICATION

Having addressed these common problems, now I'd like to offer more practical help for moving toward assurance. Below are ten questions designed to help you decide if you are entitled to assurance. (Many have been adapted from the observations of an English Puritan pastor/author of the 1600s, Thomas Brooks.)[3]

After I used these in a message recently, a single woman in her thirties who's been a Christian less than five years sent a card to me that read: "Up until last Sunday I had based my feelings of assurance on a particular incident. . . . But when I saw the list of questions you included in the outline on Sunday, I realized . . . how much I really love God . . . that I am truly a child of God—I am truly saved and nothing will ever take that away from me. And that realization continues to strengthen my assurance." If you're a child of God, may the Lord use them to strengthen your assurance too.

*Do you intensely desire assurance?* The pursuit of assurance, to most unbelievers, is about as urgent a matter as having their potassium level checked. Few of them would voluntarily read a book about assurance. So if the subject of this book means little to you, there is reason to question your salvation. Some degree of desperation about assurance, however, is a very good indication that God Himself is the author of your desire and that you do belong to Him.

*Do you sometimes grieve that you do not love Jesus enough?* Are you ever troubled by the coldness of your heart toward Christ? Do you ever groan inwardly, "Lord Jesus, I hate it when I express love for other things more than You"? Only a Christian thinks like that.

*Do you often wish God would change you so that you would always obey Him and never sin again?* Do you commonly sin and then think, *Lord, I wish You would take all of my heart and change it so that I would never sin another time?* If pretenders to Christianity were honest, they would admit to themselves that there are sins they would dearly miss and would hate to live the rest of their lives without. In contrast, those who have the Holy Spirit, despite their willful disobediences, long to be free from sin's influence. The Bible teaches that such deliverance will not happen until death or the Lord's return, but those yearning for it now are assuredly Christians.

*Do you think salvation is more important than anything else in the world?* Think carefully before you answer. No one who has read this far would say salvation is *not* important. The question is *how* important is it to you? Do you see "salvation" as something you went through as a child, or as a type of initiation ceremony in the church? Is it a significant matter to you mainly because it's important to your church, parents, spouse, children, etc.? Or is your salvation more essential to you than the perpetuation of your pulse? Despite all the family, friends, jobs, causes, and all else a Christian loves, *nothing* is more important to a Christian than his or her salvation. If everything else in your life is secondary to being right with God, accept the assurance that only those who know God persist in that outlook.

*Do you ever seriously desire to trade places with a rich, famous, or attractive person you know is not a Christian?* I'm sure even the most faithful Christians occasionally daydream of savoring the notoriety or wealth of the world's heroes. But do you ever *sincerely* wish you could exchange lives with someone such as a lottery winner, a pro sports champion, or a stunning model or movie star, even when it's obvious that the person is not a believer?

*Would you willingly and habitually sin against God if you could get whatever you wanted in return?* Christians must say no to this question, because they couldn't break the heart of God so determinedly. They know they could not stand the conviction of such a persistent choice. They could not bring themselves to spit on the Cross of Christ so unreluctantly.

*Which would you really prefer: God, Christ, the Spirit,*

*grace, glory, holiness, and Heaven; or all the money, pleasure, fame, houses, lands, possessions, and anything else you could name in this world?* Don't quickly give the answer you are expected to give. Examine your heart. Be honest. If you could have *anything* the world has to offer, and all of it you wanted for the rest of your life, would you choose it over God and the things of God? Just about everyone would say that each side has some attraction, but which is really the stronger magnet for your heart?

*Do you admire godly people more than rich, famous, athletic, or attractive people?* Who are the Christians—well known or unknown—whom you admire most? Stop and think of two or three. Now who are the wealthy, celebrated, and/or "beautiful" people who appeal to you? Of the two groups, which do you generally respect more?

*Would you be content to live without hearing sermons, praying, reading the Bible, or worshiping God in public?* I can envision some churchgoing people hearing this from a pulpit and thinking, *Frankly, if I knew I'd never hear another sermon, I wouldn't miss it a bit.* And if the truth were known, they don't pray or read the Bible much except at church, so a complete absence of these things from their lives wouldn't create much of a vacuum at all. They think God-centered worship (at any church) is boring, so it wouldn't bother them a bit were they never again able to gather with the people of God to worship Him. On the other hand, if your attitude is, "Take anything else in my life if you have to, but not these things!" then you have Spirit of God.

*Would you be willing for Christ to claim you completely as His own?* Many people want to avoid hell but don't really want to give themselves fully to Christ. Anyone who wants to be saved but plans to keep much of life partitioned from God has questionable motives at best. By contrast, no one who is outside the Kingdom of God genuinely wants the Lord to make him or her into whatever He pleases and use him or her for His glory.

One question I ask children who profess faith in Christ is, "*Why* do you want to be a Christian?" By this I hope to discover if the child has any sense of urgency about the matter or improper motives. This was a question I asked in my conversation with the seven-year-old girl recounted at the beginning of the chapter.

With an indifference that troubled me, she replied, "Because Mommy said I should."

If someone had given her assurance based on this answer, she would have had serious doubts about her salvation as a teen, or later as a mom with children of her own, if not at a much worse time—at the Judgment. Or, had she grown to live in a worldly way, she would have been a prime candidate for false assurance. As you can see, the study of assurance is no dive into the theoretical, but an intensely practical matter.

By the way, "Why do *you* want the assurance that you are going to Heaven?"

NOTES
1. C. H. Spurgeon, "Rest as a Test," *Metropolitan Tabernacle Pulpit*, vol. 47 (London: Passmore and Alabaster, 1901; reprint, Pasadena, TX: Pilgrim Publications, 1977), page 490.
2. James W. Alexander, *Consolation* (New York: Charles Scribner, 1852; reprint, Ligonier, PA: Soli Deo Gloria Publications, 1992), page 147.
3. Thomas Brooks, *The Works of Thomas Brooks*, vol. 3 (1861–67; reprint, Edinburgh: The Banner of Truth Trust, 1980), pages 288-291.

# NINE

# FALSE ASSURANCE OF SALVATION

✝

*False assurance is a more serious problem
than no assurance.*
JOHN MACARTHUR
*Faith Works*

At 7:00 a.m. on Sunday, December 7, 1941, two U.S. military officers—one naval and one army—were rising in their respective quarters. Everyone at Pearl Harbor was unprepared for what happened that morning. Most were still sleeping when the first bombs fell. These two men had planned a round of golf together. As they looked outside at the partly sunny skies and thought, *A beautiful morning for golf!*, more than 175 Japanese planes closed to within 130 miles of Oahu. But it's especially significant that the "Day of Infamy" caught these two men by surprise. One was Husband E. Kimmel, admiral over the fleet stationed at Pearl Harbor. The other was Lieutenant General Walter C. Short, commander of all military forces in Hawaii. Before they left for the course, the sky was split apart by an unexpected enemy, and nothing was ever the same again.

Many people are as falsely secure about going to Heaven as these men were about the security of Pearl Harbor. Confident they are far from any danger, they will find, one unsuspecting day, that their assurance of Heaven is blown apart, and that they themselves are sinking forever in a place much worse than the bombed and burning USS *Arizona*.

## SOURCES OF A FALSE ASSURANCE OF SALVATION

Having a false assurance of salvation is the worst mistake anyone can ever make. If a person is wrong about being right with

God and going to Heaven, ultimately it really doesn't matter what else he or she is right about.

How does it happen? What makes people think they have a good relationship with God and will spend eternity in Heaven when just the opposite is true?

## A Public Commitment or Outward Response to the Gospel

Many people think they are Christians because they made a visible, reportable response to a presentation of the gospel. They hear the biblical message of salvation, and then the preacher or evangelist says, "If you want to become a Christian, leave your seat and come to the front." Rather than "Come to Christ," the invitation is "Come forward." Instead of "Turn to the Lord Jesus and believe," it is "Turn and make your way down the aisle," or some other public response. But simply changing your location in a building doesn't make you a Christian.

Having ministered on both sides of the Atlantic, John R. de Witt sees the false assurance generated by this approach as a much greater problem pastorally than having no assurance:

> Across the Christian world spiritual birth or conversion has been placed almost on a level of a mathematical formula. That formula might be stated something like this: "When the invitation is given, go forward. If you go forward and sincerely repeat the words of a prayer of confession and faith, if you sign the commitment card, then [so we are told] you are a Christian. You may not feel like one, act like one, or have any substantial ground for considering yourself one. Nevertheless, if you have made a decision for Christ, that is all you need to do. And beyond that, you have the right to regard yourself as a fully assured child of God." I am much more concerned about this "easy believism" notion that one can be a Christian without displaying any vital signs of spiritual life than I am about an absence of assurance.[1]

Anyone who thinks he or she is on the way to Heaven simply because he or she made a public response to the gospel is falsely secure.

## Baptism

An equally common source of false assurance is baptism. In every town where I've lived, and in every country of every continent where I've preached, one of the most prevalent presumptions is that people are right with God simply because they have been sprinkled or immersed in a church ceremony. Just a few days ago in our church, a woman gave a testimony that she had been baptized as a child, but only recently realized she had never trusted Jesus Christ to take away the guilt of her sins.

Baptism is not a minor matter. Jesus, our example, was baptized (Matthew 3:13-17, Mark 1:9-11, Luke 3:21-22), and His Great Commission for the church included the command to baptize His disciples (Matthew 28:19-20). But the water of baptism on your body does not qualify your soul for Heaven. Your confidence for salvation should be in the message of the "gospel, because it is the power of God for the salvation of everyone who believes" (Romans 1:16).

Baptism has significant symbolic connections with the gospel of Jesus, but assurance should be in the Person of Christ, not in a procedure of the church.

## Involvement with Church

These professing Christians are sure of acceptance by God because they are zealously engaged in the external parts of worship and service in the church. They find it impossible to believe they could be so involved with the people and things of God for so long and not be considered part of His family. But that's like a neighbor child assuming he was part of your family just because he's often in your home and plays with your children.

The Lord Jesus warns that there's more to being right with Him than participation in the forms of religion:

> "These people honor me with their lips,
>     but their hearts are far from me.
> They worship me in vain." (Matthew 15:8-9)

I saw a horrifying news story. A member of a parachute club volunteered to videotape as a participant a jump made by the club. He leaped first, then turned the lens on the others. They floated together and finally joined hands to complete the free-falling circle. Then he taped them, one by one, as they pulled their rip cords and were jerked upright. Suddenly the image blurred as the camera swung wildly about. That was the moment the cameraman discovered he had forgotten his parachute. He had been so intent on preparing the camera and planning the filming that he had overlooked his greatest priority. Although he was as active up there as anyone else in the club and enjoyed the "fellowship," he did not realize until it was too late that he was not in the same condition as the others.

The people of God should be His most devout worshipers and most diligent workers, but no amount of worship and service will keep anyone from falling into hell.

## A Strong Christian Family Heritage

Salvation is not inherited. But many believe, because one or more parents have a strong commitment to Christ, that somehow the grace given to them covers the entire family.

Early in our ministry, Caffy and I spent dozens of evenings in the home of another couple. This pastor's wife often spoke of how well her dad "knew his Bible." Whenever we discussed theological or church matters, she typically presented what "Daddy believed" and added that "he was never wrong." Confused and embarrassed by the immoral lifestyle of her sister, she recalled how "Dad raised us right." Despite the solidity of her family's Christianity, however, it could not make her a Christian. Years ago this woman abruptly left her husband to live with another man and deny the faith of her father.

Jim, a staff member at our church, told me of a conversation at a friend's house when he was a boy. Over a bowl of popcorn, his friend's mom talked with him about the gospel and his relationship to Christ. He recalls thinking, *Of course I'll go to Heaven. My dad's a pastor.* John 3:16 proclaims, "God so loved the world that he gave his one and only Son, that *whoever believes* in him shall not perish but have eternal life" (emphasis added). Each person must believe in Christ for himself or herself. No one goes to Heaven on the spiritual coattails of another.

## An Abundance of Good Deeds

At the funeral of his grandmother, a friend of mine was told repeatedly, "If anyone is going to Heaven, she is. She lived such a good life." This kind of thinking is the most prevalent source of false assurance. People know they aren't perfect, but they also believe they do much good. So they reason, "With all the wicked people in the world, if there is any sense of fairness with God, surely He will admit the good people (like me) to Heaven." People come to this false assurance by making the most favorable comparison of all—their *good* deeds against others' *bad* deeds.

The universal error is believing that God will compare us with each other rather than against the standard of His Law. Furthermore, we all have the tendency to emphasize our good deeds and minimize our "mistakes." The problem, however, is that no matter how many good works we do, God holds us accountable for our sins.

Suppose a policeman pulled me over for speeding and ran a background check on me. He would discover that I had never been arrested, had never been to prison, etc. A pastor-friend might be in the car with me and testify that I am a wonderful family man and a good pastor, and do many things that help people. Despite all the admirable facts the officer might discover about me, he would still say, "But you are guilty of breaking the speed limit, and you must suffer the punishment for this one offense." That's our problem. No matter how many good things we do, they cannot eliminate the guilt of our sins against God's Law.

Concerning the number of our sins, imagine it was possible to commit only one sin per day. (Biblically that's impossible, but assume for the sake of argument that it could be done.) If you lived seventy years, that's more than twenty-five thousand sins! And since every sin is also a failure to keep the greatest commandment to love God with all that you are (Mark 12:28-30), the total is doubled to fifty thousand.

Then consider the weight of our sins. Every sin is against the greatest Person in the universe, which magnifies the guilt. It would be wrong to shoot at me; the law considers it a greater crime to drive by and shoot at the President of the United States. In the same way, our sins are against the Creator and King of all.

So each of us is guilty of tens of thousands of sins (if only *one* per day) against the infinitely Holy God Almighty. And some audaciously think doing good deeds will cause Him to wink at their sins and let them into Heaven. Yes, God is perfectly loving, but He is also perfectly just. If He fails to punish one sin He will no longer be perfectly just. And if He ceases to be perfect in any area, He is no longer God. The biggest fool in the world is the person who expects to stand before God and impress Him with good deeds, even "Christian" deeds.

Our only hope of salvation is in the grace of God and the work of Christ, not our works. If you could accumulate the credit of every good deed ever done in the world, it would not outweigh your sins. We must trust Another for salvation. That's why Ephesians 2:8-9 reminds us, "For it is by grace you have been saved, through faith—and this not from yourselves, it is the gift of God—not by works, so that no one can boast." There is no more widespread misconception about the Bible than the notion that it teaches we will go to Heaven if our good and righteous deeds outweigh our bad deeds on God's scale of justice.

Make sure you don't place your assurance of Heaven on a misunderstanding of the entrance requirements.

**An Extraordinary Experience**
Increasing numbers of people report "near-death" experiences, claiming they went to Heaven during moments when it appeared they were dying, but were sent back. Invariably they express assurance of going to Heaven later because of this event. On a broader scale, statistics show that many Americans testify to some kind of religious experience that has changed their lives.

I have watched people on television fall as though shot by what they said was the power of the Holy Spirit. A friend said he could "feel the electricity" at a crowded coliseum in Chicago where dozens claimed healing at the hand of a preacher. And almost anyone who attends church regularly can remember an unusually transcendent worship experience.

May a person assume assurance of good standing with God because of a vivid religious or spiritual experience? Not according to Jesus. Let's return to Matthew 7:22-23 where He said, "Many will say to me on that day, 'Lord, Lord, did we not prophesy in your name, and in your name drive out demons and perform many miracles?' Then I will tell them plainly, 'I never knew you. Away from me, you evildoers!'" Not many people can claim such exceptional religious experiences. Nevertheless, Jesus says He will turn these people away from Heaven's door. Remember, every religion can produce people with extraordinary experiences and what appear to be remarkable answers to prayer. But unless we are ready to say there is a way to God in all religions, we must say these experiences are unreliable.

Jesus said there is only one experience that matters if you want to see God in Heaven: "I tell you the truth, no one can see the kingdom of God unless he is born again" (John 3:3). How can a person know if his or her "extraordinary experience" was this new birth Jesus spoke of? Rather than be repetitive, I refer you back to chapters 3 through 5.

## A Dramatic Personal or Lifestyle Change

A person says she wants to be born again and in a crisis experience expresses faith in Christ. Afterward her life is undeniably changed. Can she be sure from this that she is a Christian?

While I would argue that change inevitably occurs in the life of a born-again person, assurance is not warranted if the changes do not conform to Scripture or do not last. The classic example of change without conversion is Judas Iscariot. His lifestyle took a dramatic turn when he became a disciple of Jesus. Talk about extraordinary experiences! He lived with God as God lived on earth. He talked with Him and saw Him do the miraculous every day. But the changes in his life were not the work of the Spirit of

God, for Jesus referred to him as "a devil" (John 6:70-71) and "the one doomed to destruction" (17:12).

Every cult and false religion is filled with followers who say their life has been changed by it. A member of our church was once in the Forum (formerly known as EST) cult. Part of the initial attraction for her was the testimonies of people whose lives were transformed by its teaching. Followers of psychics, Scientology, Mormonism, positive thinking, etc., frequently appear on television saying, "It works for me; it can work for you." For that matter, devotees of diet centers and Alcoholics Anonymous speak of being "born again" by the lifestyle changes caused by their new eating and drinking habits.

The question is not whether you have experienced change since you believed, but whether you have experienced the *lasting* changes that the *Spirit of God* makes. Those are the only changes that really matter.

**Material Blessing and Financial Security**
Some people misapply the Old Testament promises of prosperity for God's faithful and presume that their earthly blessings reflect heavenly approval. They think, *Since God has blessed me like this, how could He be my enemy? Surely He is not against me or He wouldn't have given me these things. I must be pleasing to Him because of the way He prospers me.*

Success in accumulating wealth may mean God is *not* pleased. God says in Ecclesiastes 2:26 that sometimes "to the sinner he gives the task of gathering and storing up wealth to hand it over to the one who pleases God."

Jesus never said the rich should draw spiritual assurance from their tangible blessings. Instead He rebuked the wealthy who were unconverted: "But woe to you who are rich, for you have already received your comfort" (Luke 6:24). In another place He warned those who had material riches but were "not rich toward God" (12:21).

God prospered the rich man in the story Jesus told in Luke 16:19-31. But at death he went from fortune on earth to flames in hell. There he was told, "Son, remember that in your lifetime you received your good things, while Lazarus received bad things, but now he is comforted here and you are in agony" (16:25).

After a rich young man wouldn't pay the price of discipleship for Jesus' offer of "treasure in heaven," "Jesus looked at him and said, 'How hard it is for the rich to enter the kingdom of God! Indeed, it is easier for a camel to go through the eye of a needle than for a rich man to enter the kingdom of God" (18:24-25). It is not impossible for the wealthy to be saved, for two verses later Jesus affirmed, "What is impossible with men is possible with God" (verse 27). But this much is clear: no one should draw the conclusion that God will bring him or her to Heaven just because He has prospered him or her on earth.

## A False Understanding of God

A false understanding of God is at the heart of most sources of false assurance. Most unconverted people, however unwittingly, make God in their own image, making Him like themselves. If they think they should go to Heaven, then God must think so too. If it is easy for them to forget their sins, they think it should be easy for God.

But God's perceived silence about sin now is no basis for assurance, for He says in Psalm 50:21,

"These things you have done and I kept silent;
  you thought I was altogether like you.
But I will rebuke you
  and accuse you to your face."

What a terrible and shocking moment to awaken on the other side of death to face a God who is not the grandfatherly "man upstairs," but holy, awesome, and inflexibly just.

"My God isn't like that" is the typical response of someone who has a wrong understanding of God, especially whenever that person encounters "a hard teaching" about Him. They sneer, "Who can accept it?" (John 6:60). They want a cafeteria approach to God, choosing the attributes they like and putting them together to create a God who's little more than a celestial genie. "I'm safe," they think, "God will forgive me and let me into Heaven when I die. That's His job."

"This is the frame of most men," noted John Owen,

> they know little of God, and are little troubled about any thing that relates unto him. God is not reverenced, sin is but a trifle, forgiveness a matter of nothing; whoso will have it for asking. But shall this atheistical wickedness of the heart of man be called a discovery of forgiveness? Is not this to make God an idol? [2]

True, God is perfectly loving (1 John 4:8). But He does not have love without justice. His wrath is equal to His mercy. He is perfect in every attribute. We should not want it any other way. If we get angry when a judge or referee in the Olympics shows partiality, how would we feel if God did not administer justice to all the wickedness done in the world? A right understanding of God balances all the qualities He has revealed about Himself in the Bible. But how can that be? How can He be inflexibly just toward sin and also completely forgiving? The answer is found in the Cross. There He was "just and the one who justifies those who have faith in Jesus" (Romans 3:26). In Jesus He justly punished all the sins of "those who have faith in Jesus" so He could then forgive them. Our Substitute willingly received God's wrath so we could receive His mercy.

No human could ever have conceived of such a plan. Let us draw assurance from God as He has revealed Himself in the Bible, not as our limited minds would like Him to be.

### A False Understanding of Sin and Hell

People who do not believe God will send anyone to hell, not to mention those who doubt its existence, obviously believe they will go to Heaven.

The same goes for those who think sin is a trifle and God is just like them, only without sin. Some people reason this way: "If I can go one second without sin, I can go two. If I can go two seconds without sin, I can go five. If I can go five, I can go a

minute. If I can go a minute, I can go an hour, etc." The problem
with this reasoning is in the first proposition. No one can go one
second without sin. That's because we are sinners by *nature*
(Ephesians 2:3) as well as by choice and action. To say "I can go
one second without sin" is like saying, "I can go one second
without my nature" or, "I can go one second without existing."
Sin is as much a part of our nature as our blood. So just as we
cannot say, think, or do anything without blood flowing through
our veins, neither can we say, think, or do anything without
some measure of sin.

Hell is just as misunderstood as sin. Hell must exist because
creatures who are sinful by nature cannot live in the presence of
a God who is holy by nature. Suppose you were instantly trans-
ported to the surface of the sun. What would happen? You'd be
vaporized. Why? Because your nature is incompatible with the
nature of the sun. Regarding His utter holiness, the Bible says
"our God is a consuming fire" (Hebrews 12:29). Unless a sinful
people's nature is changed into conformity with God's holy
nature (which will happen to believers when they see Christ; see
Philippians 3:20-21, 1 John 3:2-3), they cannot live with God.
They must be sent to another place.

That other place is hell. Hell is a place where the unrepentant are "punished with everlasting destruction and shut out from
the presence of the Lord" (2 Thessalonians 1:9). Some think the
descriptions of hell are symbolic. Even if that is so, remember
that symbols are only substitutes for the reality they depict. The
reality would be worse. And yet hell is infinitely worse than you
could ever imagine.

Those who deny hell's existence and think such a place is
incompatible with the character of Jesus should realize that there
is more about hell in the words of Jesus than in the rest of the
Bible put together. Actually, though, it is *merciful* of Jesus to
warn us of hell.

How would you feel if you were trying to get home on a
stormy night and saw a rain-drenched man standing in the middle
of your lane, waving his arms? Your first thoughts might be, *Oh*

*no. What does this guy want? Is he a hitchhiker? Or worse? I just want to get home. I don't want to stop for a stranger here on a dark road in a downpour.* No matter how much you veer on the highway, he keeps appearing in your headlights. Finally you either have to stop or run him down. He hurries toward your door, and cautiously you lower the window half an inch.

"The bridge has collapsed just ahead. I've been trying to flag people down. Several cars ahead of you drove past me and down into the gorge. I'm sure they're all dead."

Now how do you feel about this man? His unwelcome message and interruption into your life take on a new perspective when you discover the danger that was waiting for you in the unknown. You're glad to turn around and go a new way home. The man you wanted to avoid at first has saved your life.

So when Jesus warns us of hell, it's actually an act of mercy.

## CHARACTERISTICS OF THE FALSELY ASSURED

You've just read of ten sources of false assurance. What characterizes people who have false assurance?

### They Are Either Unconcerned or Angry When Warned About False Assurance

Spiritually healthy Christians respond with humility to the message of false assurance. They realize that self-deception is possible. Salvation means so much to them that they don't want to disregard any biblical warnings. They want to "be self-controlled and alert," for they know their "enemy the devil prowls around like a roaring lion looking for someone to devour" (1 Peter 5:8). Even if they have "full assurance," they are watchful over their souls so that they don't become lazy.

"One of the attitudes most detrimental to assurance," said Scottish theologian John Murray, "is taking salvation for granted."[3] Yet that's exactly the way some people respond to the teaching about false assurance. The possibility of false assurance never concerns them. They never take seriously the command, "Examine yourselves to see whether you are in the faith; test yourselves" (2 Corinthians 13:5).

On the other hand, some people burn with anger at anyone who suggests the need for us to examine ourselves. They veneer their spiritual insecurity with aggressiveness rather than passivity. They react to the warnings of false assurance like a Rottweiler protecting a structurally-questionable house from a building inspector. In my experience, their resistance is prompted by an unwillingness to face the painful possibility that their assurance may be built upon sand. Their attitude seems to be, "If you don't check for problems, you won't find any. Avoid questions and doubts, and all will be well." John MacArthur summarized:

> In contemporary Christianity assurance is too often either ignored, or claimed by people who have no right to it. Too many people believe they are saved merely because someone told them so. They do not examine themselves; they do not test their assurance by God's Word; they are taught that doubts about their salvation can only be detrimental to spiritual health and growth. Yet multitudes of these people give no evidence of any spiritual health or growth whatsoever.[4]

### They Are Either Legalistic or Loose with Spiritual Disciplines and Duties

Some professing Christians are like the Pharisees of Jesus' day. They derive false assurance from the legalistic practice of church involvement, good deeds, or spiritual disciplines such as Bible study, prayer, or fasting. These scriptural duties and disciplines become an end in themselves. Bible intake is measured by the number of chapters "covered" rather than by the number of life changes made. Prayers are timed. Church attendance is counted. Service is done to be seen by others. The more rigid they become, the more righteous they feel. Reliance is upon religious works instead of the work of Christ. In the end their practice differs little from those in false religions and cults whose rituals and regimens produce an aura of assurance.

By contrast, others with false assurance are very complacent in their worldliness. Other than possibly church attendance, there's little else in their lives to distinguish them even from an atheist. They pray little, never study the Bible, and serve only out of necessity or convenience. "God will understand," they say to themselves. "He knows my circumstances and how busy I am. And He knows I'm not perfect." They find it easy to rationalize their disobedience and are quick to quote what they think are "loopholes of grace" for their lack of discipleship. They ignore verses like Hebrews 12:14, which says to "Make every effort to live in peace with all men and to be holy; without holiness no one will see the Lord."

## They Are Either Very Weak in or Very Confident of Their Bible Knowledge

Here's another illustration of how those with false assurance usually fall at one of two extremes. Those who rely heavily on their baptism, Christian family heritage, or an extraordinary experience for assurance often know very little about the Bible. They have not troubled themselves to learn God's Word because they aren't impressed with the importance of it. And it is precisely because they do *not* know the Scriptures and what it says about salvation and assurance that they feel secure. They have what they want out of Christianity (at least they think they do), so why study the Bible?

The community college near us opened its doors a few years ago to a psychic fair. Our church set up a booth outside the entrance to give out literature and witness to those who attended. I drew aside and visited at length with one psychic who was absolutely sure she was going to Heaven. Her confidence was based upon her baptism and participation in her church's rituals. Her assurance was confirmed in her mind by the extraordinary experiences she had as a psychic. I asked her how she managed to integrate being a psychic with her "Christianity." She explained that the Bible character Joseph was a psychic too, and that Scripture affirmed her "gift" in many places. Of course, all this reflected an abysmal ignorance of God's Word, especially its many outright condemnations of psychic practices.

Opposite such falsely assured professing Christians are those who can display a formidable knowledge of the Bible, yet do so exclusive of Christlike living. They may speak with "the tongues of men and of angels," but the Bible says if they "have not love," they are "only a resounding gong or a clanging cymbal" (1 Corinthians 13:1). They may appear to "fathom all mysteries and all knowledge," but if they "have not love," they are "nothing" (13:2).

The Apostle Paul reminded the Corinthian Christians, "The kingdom of God is not a matter of talk but of power" (1 Corinthians 4:20). A grasp of sound doctrine is necessary for Christian maturity and full assurance, but it proves little without the power of a Christlike life behind it.

Andrew Gray's counsel is still wise: "I beseech you, when you cast up your evidences of assurance, consider how well you have done, and not how well ye have spoken." [5]

### They Have Either a Vicarious Christianity or an Overly Independent Spirit

Some with false assurance have a vicarious Christianity. They let others be deeply committed and think that somehow, by association or identification with them, they absorb some of the results of that spirituality.

This may take the form of blind loyalty to a particular minister or Christian writer. It may find expression through reliance upon the Christian commitment of another family member, particularly a spouse. They let the other person do all the Bible reading, praying, studying, etc., and assume that by being close to that person God will somehow grant them the same blessings and benefits He gives to the one who follows Him more closely.

False assurance via vicarious Christianity is a special danger for those with a strong Christian family heritage. A friend told me that her mother believes she is safe with God because of the faith of another. "For the first five years of my life, I lived in the parsonage with my grandfather, who was a pastor." She insists, "Surely that counts for something toward Heaven."

The Bible says that even the wicked Herod used to enjoy listening to John the Baptist (Mark 6:20). Many of those who shouted for the crucifixion of Jesus once "listened to him with delight" (12:37). But any assurance of Heaven that Herod or the multitudes had because of this was a big mistake.

Proximity to or preference for godly people will not make a difference at the Judgment. The gates of Heaven admit only one at time.

Over against these are the falsely assured who have an overly independent spirit. They feel little, if any, need for the local church. The public worship of God is not a priority with them. They worship "just fine" in their "own way, thank you." Gathering for Christian fellowship seems unnecessary to spiritual mavericks. Especially since "so many of those down at the church are hypocrites" anyway. They believe they're "just as good as most church people," and if church people go to Heaven, they're confident they'll make it too.

Anyone who feels certain of Heaven but separates from the local church should consider how 1 John 2:19 applies to that practice: "They went out from us, but they did not really belong to us. For if they had belonged to us, they would have remained with us; but their going showed that none of them belonged to us."

## They May Be Constantly Resisting the Truth or Never Able to Come to the Truth

Who is more deceived than those who think they are followers of Christ but constantly resist the truth of Christ? They say, "Yeah, I'm a Christian," but never read the Bible and are bored by any form of teaching or preaching. Their lives are never changed by the Scripture. God's truth is perceived as mainly "just a bunch of rules."

But those who resist the truth of God rather than love it, according to 2 Thessalonians 2:10, will perish in eternity "because they refused to love the truth and so be saved."

Opposite them are professing believers who, in the words of 2 Timothy 3:7, are "always learning and never able to come to the knowledge of the truth" (NASB). They may attend endless Bible studies, or they may just be regular listeners to sermons.

They hear and hear, but putting the Word of God into their minds is like dropping diamonds of truth into a bag with holes. And they probably aren't even aware that they have never grasped the gospel.

I met every week for six months with a man who faithfully attended Bible study and worship. He read the Scriptures daily. He learned, but he never seemed to come closer to a saving knowledge of the truth. Some people plod along like this for sixty years, assuming all is well because they hear the truth and "do their best." Worse yet, most of them never examine themselves for the evidences of faith from 1 John, something that might be used by the Spirit to show them they have no basis for their assurance.

## MORE APPLICATION

*Are you sure God accepts you and will admit you to Heaven? Why?* If you're sure of your salvation, *why* are you sure? Don't misunderstand; I want you to be sure. This book was written to strengthen the assurance of those who are entitled to it. But it is also intended to challenge those who are uncertain and to lead them to think deeply about their relationship with God. If you're sure you're a Christian, I want this book to help you articulate clearly *why* you're sure.

*Why do you believe you do not have a false assurance?* Again, this is not intended to make you doubt but to make you *think*. Do you have biblical reasons, such as were presented earlier in this book, for believing you are right with God? If so, face this question fearlessly. If you aren't sure, look to Christ and ask Him to show you the state of your soul.

If your attitude has been, "Lord, I really do think you have given me evidence of Your Spirit's presence within me, but please don't let me be deceived," that speaks well of the integrity of your assurance. That's a humble and healthy approach to the possibility of false assurance. Princeton theologian A. A. Hodge wrote, "I think the first essential mark of the difference between true and false assurance is to be found in the fact that the true works humility." [6] I'm concerned when people react to the subject of false assurance with apathy or anger. I'm encouraged when they respond with thought and humility.

*Remember that the sources of true assurance are the character of God, the work of Jesus Christ, and the truth of God's promises.* I asked an FBI agent in our church if something I'd always heard was really the truth. He confirmed that it was. Government agents learn to spot counterfeit money by becoming extremely familiar with every aspect of the real thing. If you look carefully enough at the sources of true assurance and hold on to them, you'll learn to discern what is false.

The heartbreaking tragedy about Pearl Harbor was that there was plenty of warning, but it simply went unheeded. The military had only recently installed there a new secret weapon of detection called radar. In *At Dawn We Slept*, Gordon Prange describes the sudden appearance of an unbelievably large blip on the oscilloscope. Private Joseph Lockard thought the high-tech equipment had gone haywire, but a quick check proved that the set was working perfectly. Also on duty at the radar station was Private George Elliott, and he immediately reported the enormous sighting to the Information Center.

Lieutenant Kermit Tyler, assistant to the controller on duty at the Information Center that morning, talked with Elliott. He was sure the radar had picked up a flight of B-17s arriving from California. Tyler closed the conversation with, "Well, don't worry about it." [7] So everyone went on, falsely assured of safety, never suspecting that on that peaceful and beautiful Sunday morning their lives were about to be destroyed.

You, too, have received warning. You have been warned that there is such a thing as a false sense of assurance of being safe with God and going to Heaven. You have been warned to identify where you place your hope for Heaven, and to make sure it is in the only One who can forgive you and take you to Heaven.

Don't let the peace and beauty of this day lull you into a false security. A Day is coming that will descend more suddenly and quickly than the planes upon Pearl Harbor. The falsely secure and unprepared will sink into the fire and bottomless pit of hell forever. Those who love Christ and the Day of His appearing will be rescued from the wrath of God and brought back with Him to live in true peace and indescribable joy forever.

NOTES
1. John Richard de Witt, *Doubt and Assurance*, ed., R. C. Sproul (Grand Rapids, MI: Baker, 1993; Orlando, FL: Ligonier Ministries, 1993), page 84.
2. John Owen, *The Works of John Owen*, vol. 6 (London: Johnstone and Hunter, 1850-53; reprint, Edinburgh: The Banner of Truth Trust, 1965), page 394.
3. John Murray, *The Collected Works of John Murray*, vol. 2, *Select Lectures in Systematic Theology* (Edinburgh: The Banner of Truth Trust, 1977), page 271.
4. John MacArthur, *Faith Works* (Dallas: Word, 1993), page 158.
5. Andrew Gray, *The Works of Andrew Gray* (Aberdeen, Scotland: George and Robert King, 1839; reprint, Ligonier, PA: Soli Deo Gloria Publications, 1992), page 199.
6. John Blanchard, comp., *Gathered Gold* (Welwyn, England: Evangelical Press, 1984), page 8.
7. Gordon W. Prange, *At Dawn We Slept* (New York: Penguin Books, 1981), page 501.

# TEN

# WHAT TO DO
# IF YOU'RE STILL NOT SURE

✟

*Nothing is more important for us than to know that we are
indeed the children of God. . . . You can't really enjoy the
blessings of the Christian life unless you've got this assurance.*
MARTYN LLOYD-JONES
"Abraham, Faith in Action" (taped message)

On the night before He was crucified, Jesus Christ observed
His last Jewish Passover meal with His disciples and insti-
tuted the Lord's Supper. At that meal He revealed to His closest
followers that one of them would deliver Him to His enemies.
According to Matthew 26:21, "While they were eating, he said,
'I tell you the truth, one of you will betray me.'"

Consider the response of His most devoted disciples. "They
were very sad and began to say to him one after the other,
'Surely not I, Lord?'" (verse 22).

The form of their question indicates that (except for the
secret traitor, Judas) the eleven faithful ones could not imagine
how they could ever betray Jesus. Nevertheless, there is enough
doubt planted by Jesus' statement to cause the disciples some
loss of assurance about their relationship with Him.

As established earlier, true Christians may lack assurance
about the reality and security of their relationship with the Lord.
Genuine, faithful followers of Jesus may hear Jesus' statements
in Scripture about false assurance and be deeply grieved. Their
consciences tell them there are traitorous tendencies in their own
hearts sometimes. So they may hear the warnings that many are
falsely secure in their hope of Heaven, and with grief in their
hearts ask, "Surely not I, Lord?"

What do you do at this point if you still have no assurance of salvation and of going to Heaven? What if, like the disciples of Jesus, you have been following Him for some time and yet you are troubled about your relationship with Him? The following is not a series of successive steps. Neither will the performance of them *guarantee* a sense of assurance. But if you don't have assurance, you have no reason to expect it without pursuing it. Here is sure footing from the Scriptures, as well as from the insights and pastoral experience of generations of godly men.

## DON'T TAKE FOR GRANTED THAT YOU UNDERSTAND THE GOSPEL

A 1993 survey among churchgoers suggests widespread confusion about the gospel, even among those who feel responsible to spread it. Almost half (46 percent) of those responding to the survey say they have a personal responsibility to communicate their beliefs to others. Eighty-one percent believe the Bible is accurate in all its teachings, while 94 percent assert that Jesus Christ was crucified and resurrected. But 48 percent of these same people agreed that "if people are generally good, or do enough good things for others . . . they will earn places in heaven." In other words, half of those who profess to be Bible-believing, Christ-loving, evangelistically minded churchgoers think salvation by works is possible![1] Despite all their orthodox claims, they do not understand the most basic and important thing of all—the gospel.

My experience in the ministry has also taught me that a frightening percentage of people take for granted that they understand the gospel, but when pressed to explain it they reveal a disturbing lack of clarity. Last week a woman I believe to be a new but growing Christian came to see me. "I'm embarrassed to ask this," she said bluntly, "but what is the gospel?" As it turned out, she knew what the gospel was, but simply wanted sharper definitions and to think more precisely. Such frank forthrightness is refreshing. If only more people would desire to think so clearly about the gospel.

Are you sure you know the gospel? The New Testament plainly says the gospel is the power of God for salvation

(Romans 1:16). There is a difference between knowing all the *intricacies* of the gospel and knowing its *simple essence*. But without the knowledge of its basic message, you cannot be a Christian. Even though you may have been exposed to the gospel throughout your life and had many wonderful religious experiences, if you don't know the terms of salvation, you aren't saved.

Suppose you were writing to a friend and explaining the gospel. What would you say? In some form you would have to include what the Apostle Paul wrote in 1 Corinthians 15:3-4. There he says to these Grecian Christians, "For what I received I passed on to you as of first importance: that Christ died for our sins according to the Scriptures, that he was buried, that he was raised on the third day according to the Scriptures."

This tells us that as a minimum we must understand the gospel to be a message from Scripture about personal sin, the death of Christ as payment for sin, and His victorious resurrection. To know the benefit of this message, Jesus said we must "repent and believe the good news!" (Mark 1:15).

The gospel is more than a message about God's love, Heaven, hell, the Golden Rule, or the Second Coming. Do you realize you could believe in all these things and still not be a Christian? You may have been able to quote Bible verses since you were a child, but that doesn't mean you have ever been clear on the gospel. You could accept all the facts of the Bible as true, and consciously deny nothing it teaches, and yet not be saved.

Do you understand the gospel? Do you know what sin is? Do you comprehend that sin is more than making mistakes and not being perfect? Sin is willfully choosing to do what God has commanded that you should not do. Sin is also willfully or passively *not* doing what God has commanded that you *should* do. Your sin is such an offensive and anger-producing thing to a holy God that He had to punish it. But He was willing to punish sin in the body of His own Son, Jesus Christ, so that He could receive to Himself and into Heaven all who would repent and believe in Christ. As proof that it is all true and that God had indeed accepted this one-time sacrifice for sin, He raised Jesus bodily from the dead, never to die again.

If you lack assurance about God's acceptance of you, are you sure this is the message you believed? If it is not, you have no assurance because you have never heard or never believed the message through which salvation and assurance comes.

## THINK DEEPLY ABOUT THE GOSPEL

It is possible that you really do know the gospel and are God's child, and would gain assurance if you would only think deeply about the gospel.

When was the last time, except at a Christian meeting, when you thought long and hard about the gospel? Have you *ever* done that?

Meditation like this is much more rare and difficult today because of things like portable phones and personal stereos. We seldom allow ourselves to be in a place without music or television, and as a result we do more *passive* thinking and less *active* thinking on subjects of our own choosing. But if you never contemplate the greatness of the gospel, you're much less likely to draw assurance from it.

John Murray observed, "Too frequently believers entertain far too truncated a conception of salvation, as if, for example, it consisted merely in the forgiveness of sins and freedom from its penalty." [2] The "mere" forgiveness of sins and freedom from its penalty are only a part of salvation. Think not only of them, but of great doctrines related to the gospel like adoption, election, justification, sanctification, and glorification. Not sure what they mean? That could be one reason your assurance is low. It also demonstrates your *need* to think about them. Use your concordance, a Bible dictionary, or another reference resource to guide you. Check with your pastor, Christian bookseller, or church library for something that provides direction for your thought.

Assurance is drawn from the gospel by thinking on it just as a hummingbird draws sweetness from a flower by lingering over it. Find time soon for lingering over the gospel.

## REPENT OF ALL KNOWN SIN

Sometimes we sin away our assurance. It's not that every sin quenches our assurance, or else no one would ever be assured. But if we fall back into living like an unbeliever, God often lets us feel like one, that is, like He is far away from us. As I once heard pastor and author Joel Beeke put it, "The Christian cannot experience high levels of assurance while he participates in low levels of obedience."

When sin dims our perception of our salvation, repentance restores assurance. For although God is not pleased with our sin, He is pleased with our returning, broken heart.

Don't strain to dredge up something—anything—just to have something to confess to God. He is pleased when His children are humble, not when they grovel. You need to repent if there is some sin to which you've been clinging, and if you've been trying every possible way of regaining assurance without having to forsake it. You should repent because, as Puritan minister and writer Thomas Watson concluded, "He who is conscious to himself of secret sins, cannot draw near to God in full assurance." [3] Furthermore, God "will not pour the wine of assurance into a foul vessel." [4]

When King David's sin was exposed and confessed, he learned that "a broken and contrite heart, O God, you will not despise" (Psalm 51:17). Once he had made a thorough work of repentance, God restored to him the joy of his salvation (verse 12). He will graciously and fully restore it to us, just as He did to King David, when we wholeheartedly return.

## SUBMIT EVERYTHING TO THE LORDSHIP OF CHRIST

It's one thing to treat a specific symptom or illness when you are sick, it's another to maintain general health all the time. Repenting of a particular sin is the surgery for a specific sin that's made you spiritually ill. Submitting everything in your life to the lordship of Christ is the way to maintain general spiritual health.

Everyone gets sick on occasion; some people seem to be sick almost all the time. Those who are sick all the time often need a new way of living. They may need a dietary or environmental change, better habits of personal cleanliness, etc. In the same way, some Christians have a chronic lack of assurance, not so much because of one particular sin but because they need a general change in many areas of life.

Think back to the concentric circles in chapter 8. We considered the person who realizes that major parts of her life have been added since conversion but have not been submitted to the lordship of Christ. If you suffer from a lingering lack of assurance, could it be caused by an unexamined, unsubmitted part of your life? If so, you need to live consciously Christianly in the areas where you never before sought the will of God (cf. John 14:21).

Thomas Brooks understood this when he wrote, "The more the soul is conformed to Christ, the more confident it will be of its interest in Christ." [5]

## MEDITATE MUCH ON 1 JOHN

Remember the explicit purpose of 1 John? "I write these things," we're told in 5:13, "to you who believe in the name of the Son of God so that you may know that you have eternal life." Some Christians don't have the assurance that God loves them as His own because they have overlooked this "love letter."

American public television's long-running "Masterpiece Theatre" series presented the story of an elderly European man who had lived a lonely and often unhappy life. Decades earlier he had loved a young lady and wanted to marry her. Before he could express his feelings and intentions fully, he was called into the trenches of World War I. From there he dared to reveal his heart in a letter to her, and proposed marriage. But he never received a response. He was so heartbroken that he could never think of marrying anyone else.

He returned from the war to find her wedded to another man and living in another village. Occasionally he would see her and imagine what might have been. But he never got over her rejection, and spent most of his time in the isolation of his small farm.

One day very late in his life, the man sat on a bench and

talked with an old woman. She had known both him and his sweetheart throughout the years and was back in the village for a funeral. Always eager to hear about his old flame, he asked his friend for news of her. After speaking of her a bit, the elderly woman asked, "Why did you just leave her behind and never marry her?"

The poor farmer's face saddened as he told the story of writing and baring his heart, of longing to marry her, and of being crushed by her silence. He sighed as he said how much he had loved her all of his life and how he loved her still.

The woman paused for a long time before asking, "Are you sure you never received a letter from her?" He trembled with emotion as he said, "If I had ever gotten one message from her, I would have read it every day for the rest of my life." From a pocket inside his coat he carefully pulled a lock of her hair and a photograph with its edges worn soft. "I have kept them with me all these years," he said quietly, "and I look at them every day." Several moments passed again before the woman could say, "I was going to the post office, and I mailed her reply to you myself. Your letter made her so happy. She wrote back opening her soul to you, telling you how deeply she loved you, and that she couldn't wait to marry you. Didn't you get the letter?"

Of course he had not. And like him, having never received another letter, the young woman lost all assurance of his love.

God has written the letter of 1 John to those "who believe in the name of the Son of God." It has the expressed purpose of assuring them of His love and of His plans for them to spend eternity together. If you are in doubt of your relationship with God, don't neglect that letter. Read it over and over until God begins to warm your heart with assurance. Prayerfully survey your life in light of passages such as 2:3-5, 3:5-6, 3:14, 3:22, 5:2, and 5:11-13.

Theologian R. C. Sproul put it succinctly: "If faith comes by hearing and hearing by the Word of God, likewise assurance comes by hearing the Word of God. As I meditate on the Scriptures, my assurance is strengthened." [6] And that's especially true about meditation on the part of God's Word specifically written to give assurance.

## DON'T DOUBT THE PROMISES OF GOD

Be careful of refusing the assurance God offers to you through His promises. Spurgeon chided those who require more than this for assurance: "They have believed in the Lord Jesus, and they have his promise that they shall be saved, but they are not content with this—they want to get assurance, and then they suppose they shall have a better evidence of their salvation than the bare word of the Saviour." [7]

Look again at the "bare word of the Saviour" in John 3:16— "God so loved the world that he gave his one and only Son, that whoever believes in him shall not perish but have eternal life." *Whoever*—no matter what your age, regardless of how much sin in your life, despite your background or previous religious understanding—whoever believes *has* eternal life.

Take assurance from the promise of God in Romans 10:9— "If you confess with your mouth, 'Jesus is Lord,' and believe in your heart that God raised him from the dead, you will be saved." Not *might* be saved. *Will* be saved!

God has not said, "Seek me in vain" (Isaiah 45:19). Are you earnestly seeking Him? Believe His promise "that he rewards those who earnestly seek him" (Hebrews 11:6).

## BELIEVE AS BEST YOU CAN AND PRAY FOR GREATER FAITH

For many without assurance, the doubt is not with the truth of God's promises. What they doubt is their faith in the promises. They say, "I'm sure that whoever believes will have eternal life. I'm just not sure that I've believed. I *want* to believe, but have I?"

Some in this predicament look back to an experience from long ago and attempt to analyze it from a distance. They try to remember what they felt, thought, did, understood, and maybe even the exact words they prayed. They agonize over whether the faith they expressed then was "real" faith. But in doing so they are like a man who thinks the way to prove he's alive is to find his birth certificate.

The place to look for evidence of life is the present. It's

more important to find the signs of the Spirit in your life today than in the past. If you see them, you have biblically believed. If you're not sure, then believe as best you can and ask God to increase your faith.

Jesus was talking to a man about believing in Him when the man blurted in response, "I do believe; help me overcome my unbelief!" (Mark 9:24). To a greater or lesser degree, this man described the faith of every Christian. The sin in us keeps even the best of us from perfect faith. This is why I said in chapter 2 that it is normal for a genuine Christian to have occasional doubts about the genuineness of his or her salvation.

Additionally, this man models the spirit every Christian should have when uncertain about his or her own faith. If unsure you've believed in Christ, believe the best you know how and ask God to overcome your unbelief. If you want to believe "better," you *would* do so if you could, right? Since by your own power you can't have more faith than you do now, all you can do is believe as you're able and ask the Lord to strengthen anything that's lacking.

The wisdom of this approach is that it keeps your focus on God and not on the perceived flaws in your faith. To look too much at your faith is to look too much at yourself. Give your gaze to Christ and the Cross, and only a glance at your faith.

## PRACTICE THE SPIRITUAL DISCIPLINES

God doesn't just throw assurance into a passive heart. He requires that we cultivate assurance through the faithful use of the means of grace that He has given to us. He commands believers in 1 Timothy 4:7 to "discipline yourself for the purpose of godliness" (NASB). Part of godliness is knowing that you belong to God.

These God-given means of grace are what Christians have called the spiritual disciplines. "The Spiritual Disciplines are those personal and corporate disciplines that promote spiritual growth. They are the habits of devotion and experiential Christianity that have been practiced by the people of God since biblical times."[8] They include all forms of Bible intake, as well as prayer, individual and corporate worship, evangelism, serving, stewardship of time and money, fasting, silence and solitude, jour-naling, learning, and more.

I'm not saying you have to engage in all these before you can expect assurance. But some of them, particularly Bible intake, prayer, worship, and serving, are more closely related to assurance than others. It amazes me how people will cut them-selves off from these means of assurance and then wonder why they don't have it. "Without the diligent use of means," reasoned Thomas Brooks, "a lazy Christian has no right to expect to receive assurance." [9]

The best way to make sure there is fire in a match is to move it to action. Likewise, the best way to prove that the fire of the Holy Spirit is in you is to move into spiritual action. If there is a fire under the ashes in a fireplace, the way to find out is to fan it. "For this reason I remind you to fan into flame the gift of God, which is in you," the Apostle Paul charged Timothy (2 Timothy 1:6). Life is seen in a tree through its leaves and fruit, not in the barren branches of winter. Practice the spiritual disciplines so that the grace of God on the inside can be seen on the outside. When you see the fire and fruit of the Holy Spirit in your life, your assurance will be brighter and more full.

Note Brooks again: "Grace is most discernible when it is most in action. . . . Were your grace more active, it would be more visible; and were your grace more visible, your assurance would be more clear and full." [10]

### IF YOU REALLY LOVE GOD, TAKE ASSURANCE BECAUSE NONCHRISTIANS DON'T LOVE GOD PASSIONATELY

There is no such thing as a natural love for God. In fact, by nature we are haters of God (Romans 8:5-8, 1 Corinthians 2:14, Ephesians 2:1-3). Of course, very few people ever consider themselves haters of God. Most might even say they love God, but by God's defini-tion of love, it is plain that they do not (1 John 4:20, 5:3).

That's why one of the best indications that you know God is an abiding, sacrificial, demonstrable love for God. "The man who loves God is known by God" (1 Corinthians 8:3). You know in your deepest heart whether your love of God is just a notion or your supreme passion, and if you find your most satisfying pleasure in God. If this is the way your heart is bent, then it has been changed by the grace of God. Such affection for God is not natural; it's supernatural.

You may feel that you don't love God as you should, and for that reason question your salvation. But do you wish you *could* love Him perfectly? Does it grieve you that you do not love Him with all your heart, soul, mind, and strength? Unconverted people don't think like that.

One of the most influential thinkers in church history was the fourth-century North African, Augustine. He said a person may love gold, even though the person has none, but no one loves God who does not have Him. Do you love God?

## IF YOU HATE YOUR SIN, TAKE ASSURANCE BECAUSE NONCHRISTIANS DON'T HATE SIN DEEPLY

Just as nonChristians don't love God passionately, so they do not hate their sin deeply. They may be annoyed at the trouble it gets them into. They may be disappointed or upset by failing to meet their own standards of performance. But that is very different from the Christian attitude of hating sin because it offends God and of despising your own heart when it leads you away from God.

Christians acknowledge that to be made in the image of God is good; they don't say the human body is evil. Still, there are times when Christians cry out with Paul in Romans 7:24, "What a wretched man I am! Who will rescue me from this body of death?" Christians ache for the day of deliverance from their own sinful desires.

Paul described the internal warfare with sin that begins with the introduction of the Holy Spirit into a soul: "The sinful nature desires what is contrary to the Spirit, and the Spirit what is contrary to the sinful nature. They are in conflict with each other, so that you do not do what you want" (Galatians 5:17). Christians will often choose to sin because the tentacles of sin still cling to their hearts and reach into their minds. And yet they will cry out afterward, "Lord, forgive me! I *hate* what I did. Why do I keep doing it? Please take that desire away from me. I wish you would change me so I would never do that again." There will also be times when temptation will make your heart feel like lead because of the desire to sin, yet the Spirit will cause you to resist.

What many Christians fail to see is that this war with sin is testimony to the saving presence of the Spirit within them. The insightful Puritan John Owen put it this way: "Your state is not at all to be measured by the opposition that sin makes to you, but by the opposition you make to it." [11] Don't judge whether you are saved simply by how much sin fights against you, even when you feel saturated with sin. The question is, "How much do you hate it and fight back?" Instead of being devastated by the presence of sin, take assurance from your hostility against it.

## IF YOU'VE NEVER BEEN BAPTIZED, PRESENT YOURSELF AS A CANDIDATE IN OBEDIENCE TO CHRIST

It's one thing to misunderstand what the New Testament teaches about baptism, but it's another to be presented with Jesus' command and example of baptism and to reject it. If you can read the Great Commission of Jesus in Matthew 28:19-20 along with the other New Testament passages about baptism and still refuse to be baptized, you *should* struggle with assurance of salvation.

In 1 Peter 3:21 baptism is related to "a good conscience toward God." Don't expect to pass it by without consequences in your conscience. This one act of disobedience can mean the difference between having and not having assurance.

A few months ago I baptized someone who had been procrastinating for more than a year. The longer she delayed, the more she wondered about the reality of her salvation. But immediately afterwards her spiritual life accelerated. Family members and unbelieving friends both commented on the change in her life. Her relationship with Christ deepened and her impact for Him broadened. Spiritually she felt freed and empowered in new ways.

If you think you have repented and believed in Christ, present yourself to your church as a candidate for baptism.

## DON'T NEGLECT THE LORD'S SUPPER

Jesus also gave us another ordinance by command and example, the Lord's Supper (Luke 22:14-20, 1 Corinthians 11:23-34). In it "the promises of God are made visible." [12] Ignoring this memorial to Him, or willfully neglecting its regular observance, may diminish assurance.

It is so important to take the Lord's Supper and take it in a worthy manner that Paul says in 1 Corinthians 11:30 some in the Corinthian church were allowed to become weak, sick, and even to die because they did not approach it seriously enough. If it's so important to the Lord that He would allow serious physical consequences like this, it's no wonder that some may suffer from a lack of assurance for the same offense.

In the classic Puritan work on assurance, *Heaven on Earth*, Thomas Brooks reported a routine that's as common in our day as it was in his 350 years ago:

> Many precious Christians there are that have lain long under fears and doubts, sighing and mourning; that have run from minister to minister, and from one duty to another, &c., and yet could never be persuaded of the love of Christ to their poor souls; but still their fears and doubts have followed them, *till they have waited upon the Lord in this glorious ordinance,* by which the Lord hath assured them of the remission of their sins, and the salvation of their souls.[13] (emphasis added)

The Lord's Supper is the sign Christ has given us of His death. It is precious to Him. If you want assurance, let what is precious to Him be precious to you.

## DON'T COMPARE EARTHLY FATHERS
## TO YOUR HEAVENLY FATHER

Growing numbers of people find it hard to believe that God loves and accepts them because their earthly father didn't. Their father, stepfather, or other authority figure may have abused them verbally, physically, or sexually. This usually results either in greater difficulty trusting God or else feeling unlovable and unacceptable.

A deacon's wife confided in me that she had a longstanding uncertainty about her relationship with God. Despite all I offered, nothing seemed to help. Months later she told me she finally resolved her doubts, but only after facing the problems of abuse by her father. She realized she could not let him represent her view of her heavenly Father.

Even the person with the best of earthly fathers has an imperfect example of God's love. So each of us must learn to take our view of God from His self-revelation in the Bible, and not associate the sins of others with His character.

What is the true character of the Father? Jesus Christ said, "I and the Father are one" (John 10:30), and "Anyone who has seen me has seen the Father" (14:9). That means the heavenly Father is as tenderly loving and accepting of the abused as Jesus was of the outcast and almost certainly abused woman at the well of Samaria in John 4.

## SEEK GODLY COUNSEL IF THE DOUBTS PERSIST

If you've read this far and still your assurance drags with doubt, have the courage to talk with your pastor or a mature Christian friend about it. Don't keep lying sleepless in the night, anguished with fears about eternity, without getting help.

"Pride only breeds quarrels," states Proverbs 13:10, "but wisdom is found in those who take advice." The same book also insists, "Listen to advice and accept instruction, and in the end you will be wise" (19:20). Obviously, you shouldn't get just anyone's advice, but *godly* counsel. Talk to one or more people who know the Scriptures and can give you wise guidance. Go elsewhere if someone flippantly says, "Of course you're a Christian! What gives you the silly idea that you're not?"

I realize it could be difficult for you to make that step. You may have professed to follow Christ for a long time. Others may consider you a leader in the church and be shocked that you could doubt your salvation. But don't let pride or fear keep you from seeking assurance. Consider that your soul, your eternity, and Heaven and hell, are all at stake.

## PRAY FOR ASSURANCE

As basic as it may sound, have you ever prayed, "Lord, please give me assurance"? Have you pleaded earnestly and regularly for assurance? You may have thought about the matter during sermons or while reading this book, but have you simply asked God to grant you assurance? "How strange is it," asked Andrew Gray, "that many are so seldom on their knees complaining of their uncertainty?"[14] Say to Him, "Lord, I'm struggling with whether I'm Your child. I'm not sure I've really believed. Would You show me the true condition of my heart and where I stand with You? If I'm not a Christian, please make that clear to me. If I am, would You give me the full assurance spoken of in the Bible?" If you do not have assurance, could it be that "you do not have, because you do not ask God" (James 4:2)?

## WAIT PATIENTLY UPON GOD TO GIVE YOU A FULLER EXPERIENCE OF ASSURANCE

The Westminster Confession of Faith says of assurance, "A true believer may wait long, and conflict with many difficulties, before he be partaker of it."[15] If you have done all you know to do and still don't have assurance, then stay faithful, keep praying, and *wait*.

While waiting, Thomas Brooks recommended, "Don't sit down discouraged, be up and doing."[16] Don't wait passively. Assurance is often like a seed. It takes time to grow. Your job is to remove any weeds (sins) that could hinder its growth. You should water it with the Word of God and prayer, and cultivate it with other spiritual disciplines. But only God can make it grow.

God often gives this testimony to the person who has waited in a pit of despair about assurance:

I waited patiently for the LORD;
    he turned to me and heard my cry.
He lifted me out of the slimy pit,
    out of the mud and mire. (Psalm 40:1-2)

Maybe you're still in a "slimy pit" of "the mud and mire" of uncertainty. I can't tell you how many days, months, or years of waiting God may require. But no matter how long it is, Brooks was right: "God never hath failed, and never will fail the waiting soul. . . . Assurance is a jewel worth waiting for." [17]

## MORE APPLICATION

*Assurance is a gift of God and will not come by your efforts; nevertheless, it will not come without your efforts.* One day Jesus asked His disciples who people were saying He was. They told Him some thought He was John the Baptist come back to life, or Elijah, Jeremiah, or one of the prophets. Then He stunned them: "'But what about you?' he asked. 'Who do you say I am?'" When Simon Peter answered, "You are the Christ, the Son of the living God," Jesus responded with, "Blessed are you, Simon son of Jonah, for this was not revealed to you by man, but by my Father in heaven" (Matthew 16:13-17).

It is the same with assurance. God, by His Holy Spirit, reveals to His own the assurance that they are His. Any Christian who experiences true assurance does so as a gift of God's grace.

But that doesn't mean we are to do nothing, lounging laissez-faire in hopes that God will zing us with assurance. "Remember, Christians," said Brooks, "that the want of the exercise in grace is the reason why you do not discern your grace, and why you have no more assurance of your future happiness." [18]

*Will you persevere in Christian living and the pursuit of God even if you never get assurance?* In a sermon published in 1652, an Old English Puritan named Anthony Burgess suggested that God sometimes withholds assurance so that we might taste and see how bitter sin is. He keeps assurance from some in order to keep them from spiritual pride. With others He waits to give assurance so that when He does give it, they will prize it all the more and never take it for granted the way some do. There are cases where He delays assurance so that as His children continue to obey Him by faith, He is honored all the more. Then there are those believers who must wait long for assurance so that through their experience they may be able to comfort others who believe but lack assurance.[19] If God still has not given you assurance, perhaps Burgess has revealed His reason. Regardless, the key question is not "What is God doing?" but "What will *you* do?" Will you continue to obey God and seek God and live for God, even if He never gives you assurance?

To keep living by faith like this and not by spiritual feelings is in itself a good evidence of salvation. Who would continue to live like a son or daughter of God, even though he or she aches for assurance of God's love, except a child of God? Who would keep hungering for the things of the Spirit except one in whom the Spirit of God lives? Who would want to keep persevering toward Heaven when he or she had no assured sense of going there except one who was born from above and a citizen of Heaven?

If the cause of a lack of assurance is Satanic attack, trials, harsh circumstances, illness, temperament, or God's withdrawal of a sense of His presence, then perseverance is the most important thing you can do in the pursuit of assurance. Though your soul suffers much in the quest and God never grants assurance to you, be like Job at his best. When God had allowed him to lose his family, wealth, and health, Job exclaimed, "Though he slay me, yet will I hope in him" (Job 13:15).

God is a good God and loves to grant assurance. Suppose someone told your young child that he or she legally belonged to someone else. How would you respond if that child anxiously asked for assurance that he or she was really yours? Do you think your heart goes out to comfort your children more than God's great and perfect heart does toward His? True, sometimes He does wait to grant assurance. But our gentle and wise

Father has reasons only of love when He allows His children to be without a sense of assurance. So don't doubt His goodness or compassion. If through love He was willing to let His Son die for His enemies and sinners, will He long withhold assurance from them when now they love His Son? I give the final word to Thomas Brooks:

> If you would strengthen and maintain your assurance, then *see to it that your hearts run more out to Christ than to assurance*; to the sun than to the beams, to the fountain than to the stream, to the root than to the branch, to the cause than to the effect, Song of Solomon 1:13. Assurance is sweet, but Christ is more sweet. Assurance is lovely, but Christ is altogether lovely, Song of Solomon 5:16. Assurance is precious, but Christ is most precious. . . . Therefore let thy eye and heart, first, most, and last, be fixed upon Christ, then will assurance bed and board with thee.[20]

NOTES

1. "Poll Shows Confusion Over Gospel Message," *Moody*, October 1993, page 67.
2. John Murray, *The Works of John Murray*, vol. 2, *Select Lectures in Systematic Theology* (Edinburgh: The Banner of Truth Trust, 1977), page 270.
3. Thomas Watson, *A Body of Divinity* (1692; reprint, Edinburgh: The Banner of Truth Trust, 1970), page 257.
4. Watson, page 257.
5. John Blanchard, comp., *Gathered Gold* (Welwyn, England: Evangelical Press, 1984), page 7.
6. R. C. Sproul, *The Soul's Quest for God* (Wheaton, IL: Tyndale, 1992), page 217.
7. C. H. Spurgeon, "The True Position of Assurance," *Metropolitan Tabernacle Pulpit*, vol. 10 (London: Passmore and Alabaster, 1865; reprint, Pasadena, TX: Pilgrim Publications, 1981), page 549.
8. Donald S. Whitney, *Spiritual Disciplines for the Christian Life* (Colorado Springs, CO: NavPress, 1991), page 15.
9. John Blanchard, comp., *More Gathered Gold* (Welwyn, England: Evangelical Press, 1986), page 12.
10. Thomas Brooks, *Heaven on Earth* (1654; reprint, Edinburgh: The Banner of Truth Trust, 1961), page 150.
11. John Owen, *The Works of John Owen*, vol. 6 (London: Johnstone and Hunter, 1850-53; reprint, Edinburgh: The Banner of Truth Trust, 1965), page 605.

12. Joel R. Beeke, *Assurance of Faith*, American University Studies, Series 7: Theology and Religion, vol. 89 (New York: Peter Lang, 1991), page 179.
13. Brooks, pages 27-28.
14. Andrew Gray, *The Works of Andrew Gray* (Aberdeen, Scotland: George and Robert King, 1839; reprint, Ligonier, PA: Soli Deo Gloria Publications, 1992), pages 192-193.
15. The Westminster Confession of Faith, 18:3 (Glasgow, Scotland: Free Presbyterian Publications, 1985), page 77.
16. Brooks, page 316.
17. Brooks, page 316.
18. Brooks, page 151.
19. Anthony Burgess, *Spiritual Refining* (London: A. Miller, 1652; reprint, Ames, IA: International Outreach, 1990), pages 35-37.
20. Brooks, page 307.

# AUTHOR

✝

DONALD S. WHITNEY is an associate professor of biblical spirituality at the Southern Baptist Theological Seminary in Louisville, Kentucky, and is currently completing a ThD at the University of South Africa. He is the author of *Spiritual Disciplines for the Christian Life*, *Ten Questions to Diagnose Your Spiritual Health*, and *Simplify Your Spiritual Life* (all NavPress). Don holds a doctor of ministry degree from Trinity Evangelical Divinity School in Deerfield, Illinois, and was previously a professor of spiritual formation at Midwestern Baptist Theological Seminary in Kansas City, Missouri, for ten years. Don's wife, Caffy, ministers from their home as a women's Bible study teacher, an artist, and a freelance illustrator. The Whitneys are parents of a daughter, Laurelen Christiana. You may subscribe to Don's free e-mail newsletter at his website, www.BiblicalSpirituality.org.

# STRENGTHEN YOUR WALK WITH HELP FROM DONALD S. WHITNEY.

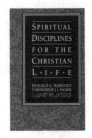

## Spiritual Disciplines for the Christian Life

Donald S. Whitney
ISBN-13: 978-0-89109-772-3
ISBN-13: 0-89109-772-4

Drawn from the church's rich heritage, this book will guide you through disciplines that can deepen your walk with God including Scripture reading, evangelism, fasting, journaling, and stewardship.

To get your copies, visit your local bookstore, call
1-800-366-7788, or log on to www.navpress.com.

NAVPRESS